THE TIME OF YOUR LIFE

The Time of Your Life

CHOOSING A VIBRANT, JOYFUL FUTURE

MARGARET TRUDEAU

HARPER**AVENUE**

Published by Harper Avenue, an imprint of HarperCollins Publishers Ltd.

First Edition

HarperCollins Publishers Ltd
2 Bloor Street East, 20th Floor
Toronto, Ontario, Canada
M4W 1A8

www.harpercollins.ca

Library and Archives Canada Cataloguing in Publication
information is available upon request

ISBN 978-1-44343-183-5

Printed and bound in the United States

RRD 9 8 7 6 5 4 3 2 1

This book is dedicated to my extraordinary, huge family—all of you.
With our shared love, all is possible.

CONTENTS

MAKE THIS REMAINING TIME COUNT

The rest of your life is here: now is the time to prepare.

I have been many things in my life: wife, mother, advocate for brain health, friend, flower child, outcast. But one thing I have never been is a long-range planner.

There are many reasons for this, not least of which is the fact that I live with bipolar disorder—a mood disorder that, among other things, affects one's ability to fully understand consequences. When you don't think about consequences, why would you plan for the future? As a result, in many ways I've lived my life as a perpetual teenager—fully and completely in the moment.

At its best, my passion for the present has given me a joie de vivre and an ability to savour the various phases of my life. But I have sometimes been incredibly, exuberantly happy, and other times, despairingly sad. For better or worse, I've lived those experiences moment by moment. But at its worst, my attachment to the present has blinded me to forces looming on the horizon—aging, for example. Until recently, I never thought about getting older and how it might affect my life. Get old? That's what other people did. In my mind, you see, I was still a worldly 19-year-old—albeit with a lovely condo and adorable grandchildren.

Then one day I woke up and I was 65. And in the space of a few short months, three events occurred that would dramatically alter how I saw myself and the precious time I have left.

The first event seemed innocuous enough, at first. It was winter 2012, and I was skiing with my eldest grandson on a bunny hill at Morin-Heights outside Montreal. My sons Justin and Sacha have a chalet in the Laurentians, and I was spending the weekend there with Sacha and his family. I was supremely happy that day. I was doing one of the things I love most in the world—skiing—with one of the people I love most in the world—my dear little Pierre. We had a few runs under our belts and were just getting off the chairlift for another when I tipped and crashed into the ice, shoulder-first. It wasn't a dramatic skiing accident—I've experienced far worse. But it was enough to dislocate my shoulder, again. (I had suffered a similar injury a few years earlier.) For some months after my fall at Morin-Heights, I was barely able to lift my arm. To this day, the joint aches anytime I get cold or lift something heavy. But the worst part of all is that the injury was enough to bar me from skiing. One small miscalculation and the enduring hobby of my life—an activity that has given me countless years of pleasure—was seemingly lost to me. Fortunately, after two years of healing, I will ski again.

The second event, a few months later, was even more devastating. My mother passed away. Her health had been failing for many years, and my sisters and I had been bracing for her death for some months. But all the preparation in the world can't prevent the aching grief of losing someone who means so much to you. I missed my mother terribly and experienced her death as a great unmooring, as though the strings that attached my 65-year-old body to my childhood self were finally cut. As long as she was around, I was still somebody's child. Now, with both my parents gone, I was not only an orphan, I was suddenly an elder.

For a long time after my mother's death, I found myself reflecting on her final years, and how much the aging process had changed her. Mum was always a bold, strong-willed, independent woman. Years before the women's liberation movement, she had insisted my father pay her for her work as a stay-at-home mother. She diligently invested her earnings in energy stocks, so that at the time of her passing she had a sizable estate. She was comfortable and well cared for to the end. But financial stability couldn't give her what she lost in her last years, when her health failed and her friends disappeared one by one: a zest for life. She told me once, a few years before she died, that she wished her life would just end. "You can't mean that, Mum," I chided her. But in my heart I knew she *did* mean it. For my mother, and for many other women of her generation, aging was an act of gradual disappearance, not a bang but a whimper. And so she faded away—in spirit and in body—for years before she finally left us. Her death brought me face to face, for the very first time, with my own mortality.

Soon after came the third event, when one of my best friends was diagnosed with Alzheimer's disease. She and I once spent long hours chatting over good coffee, discussing books we'd read and places we'd visited, fantasizing about adventures that still lay before us. Now I visit her in a nursing home. I do most of the talking. Every once in a while she pipes up and tries to convince me to move in. "We could have rooms side by side! And you don't have to worry about a *thing* here." This is hilarious and sad at the same time.

Taken together, my injury, my mother's death and my friend's diagnosis had a powerful effect on me. These experiences convinced me that I did not want to spend the last months or years of my life withering, waiting to die or in any way being less than who I was. But in the wake of so much loss, I wasn't certain how to cope.

I fell into a slump. I allowed my grooming to slip and stayed inside my apartment. Why bother keeping up appearances? I was officially an old woman. One evening, while watching an episode of *Game of Thrones*, I heard one of the characters describe the three stages of womanhood as maid, mother and crone. I wanted to throw something at the television. Maidenhood, in the Shake-spearean sense, was decades behind me, as were my childbearing years. Which left only one option. A *crone*! How awful, I thought, miserably. What do crones have to look forward to other than mushy food and leather-bound back issues of *Reader's Digest*?

Over the ensuing months, I let myself wallow in a post-midlife melodrama. My family became concerned that I was falling into a depressive state. I loved them for their concern. I have battled interwoven bouts of depression and mania my entire adult life. But it wasn't depression I was suffering from; it was a sense of restlessness. I had a dreadful fear that my best years were behind me and that my most important future contributions to the world could be summed up in two words: free babysitting.

And then one afternoon I had an epiphany. I was sitting on the couch in my living room, looking through old photographs and reliving my blithe, carefree years of maidenhood and motherhood. I saw photographs of myself in designer clothes and expensive furs, travelling the globe as the first lady of Canada. In other photos I saw my unlined face laughing into the camera, surrounded by baskets of produce I'd grown at the summer home I once enjoyed at Harrington Lake. In still others I danced with Andy Warhol. The events had happened an eternity ago, and yet I remembered the circumstances of each photograph as vividly as if it were yesterday. A thought passed through my mind: I'm never going to have a little bookstore in a country village in England. Followed by another one: I guess I'll never be a great actress.

I shoved the photo albums onto the coffee table and started listing all the things I would probably never do. It's possible that I cried, thinking these things. (I did warn you about my inner teenager.) But as I wrote, a strange thing happened: the longer my list grew, the lighter I felt. Because at some point I realized that, in fact, my chances of becoming an Olympic skier *were* firmly behind me. I really *was* 65. I had fifteen, possibly twenty years of good health ahead of me. When you are sixteen, fifteen years feels like an eternity. When you are 65, it feels like a summer—sufficient, but wouldn't it be grand if it were longer? Something I can only describe as a profound determination rose up inside me. I had to make this remaining time *count*. And for the first time in my life it dawned on me that to truly savour the moment, I would have to start planning for the future.

When I left my first husband, Pierre Trudeau, I told him it was because I wanted to be free. We had a great love between us, but we were doomed from the start. There was the age difference, of course—twenty-nine years. But it was more than that. I was a free-spirited hippie who yearned for wide-open spaces. He was disciplined and austere, and as prime minister of Canada, virtually had the weight of the nation on his shoulders. "I don't need any of your money, I don't need anything—I just want to be free," I told him as I prepared to walk out the door. I have never forgotten his condescending reply: "But, Margaret—with freedom comes great responsibility."

For years after that, I couldn't bear the responsibility of freedom. I wanted to, but I couldn't. My lifelong illness, which I wrote about in my memoir *Changing My Mind*, was partly to blame. I battled bipolar disorder unsuccessfully for years, and it wasn't until I was well into middle age that I truly developed the skills and found the support to manage the illness. Because of this struggle, I didn't really mature until I was in my fifties, and as a result, I spent years of my adult life doubting my ability to be truly responsible (even as I raised five children, volunteered, wrote books and worked). When I realized that I would need to begin planning for my future, those old insecurities reared up inside me again. So I did what I have learned to do anytime I start to doubt my resilience: I talked to my friends.

Usually such conversations have a calming effect. But when it came to discussions around preparing for old age, I realized that many of my friends were as ill-prepared as I was. We had simply forgotten to think about the future. And in many cases, the friends who thought they were prepared had been confronted with crises that threw them into devastation and uncertainty. A couple I know—she a lawyer and her husband an architect—had both committed most of their adult lives to their careers with the plan of spending their retirement travelling. But shortly after retiring, he developed severe dementia. Just like that, their best-laid plans dramatically unravelled.

The more conversations I had, the more I realized just how unprepared most of us are—as individuals and as a society—for the great grey-volution. According to Statistics Canada, between 2006 and 2011 the number of people aged 60 to 64 in Canada rose by 29.1 percent, faster than any other age group. In some jurisdictions, public transit organizations are putting an end to the practice of offering seniors discounts because there are simply too many of us. Because of this dramatic shift, the Canadian Life and Health Insurance Association estimates the nation will require at least $1.2 trillion in long-term care programs. That's because as we get older, a number of factors can negatively impact our quality of life—chronic or acute disease, disabilities, cognitive and mobility losses, and psychological problems including social isolation.

Meanwhile, in nursing schools, only 8 percent of clinical hours have a gerontological focus. Spending on aging research and supports is on the rise, but many of the experts I consulted while writing this book suggest that our society is vastly unprepared for the dramatic social and economic implications of having so many people getting older at exactly the same time.

Does this scare you? It certainly worried me. It's not that any of this was news. We've been listening to dire warnings about aging baby boomers for years. But the concurrence of events that happened in my sixty-fifth year made it so very real to me. And the more I researched, the more I realized that making my last decades of great health count isn't merely a personal mission—it's a social imperative. There are simply not enough young people to support us all. As much as I adore my children, I do not wish to rely on them in my old age. I have spent years of my life held captive variously by marriage, mental illness and public scrutiny. It was at great cost that I won back my personal freedom. I'm in no rush to hand it over once more to someone else—even if it *is* to my beloved offspring. So how then can I maintain my freedom, sense of wonder and agency in my own life, given the complications that lie ahead? How will any of us?

I certainly don't have all the answers, but I know this to be true: we have a great degree of control over what happens to us in the last third of our lives. Gerontologists call it the "life course"— the trajectory we set for ourselves as we age, based on how we choose to live our lives today. What that life course might look like is exactly what we are about to explore together.

CHAPTER 1

DO IT NOW

Reinvent what it means to age.

From the civil rights movement to women's liberation, my generation has had a profound impact on the social order. When I was a young woman, the overarching expectation was that once you became pregnant, it was time to quit working—indefinitely. Today many employers offer mothers *and* fathers parental leave, so that they can care for their babies and also maintain a professional life. The fight for these hard-won freedoms started long before my time, but our generation brought them home. Now we are poised to redefine what it means to age.

We cannot look to previous generations for guidance—they didn't face the same demographic complications we do, nor did they have the same expectations of their older years. So ordinary people like you and I must join thousands of researchers across the developed world who are scrambling to figure out precisely what a sustainable, vibrant life looks like for people north of 50. In other words, as we approach what Jane Fonda calls the "third act" of our lives, we must reinvent ourselves.

This is something I happen to know a great deal about. I have lived through two divorces, the loss of a son, mental illness and several career changes, most of it in the public eye. Now I find myself on a new odyssey—accepting still more change and examining all the possibilities that lie before me. Reinventing what it means to age means reinventing myself yet again. I choose to see both freedom and opportunity in that.

But reinvention isn't easy. In fact, personal change is one of the hardest things in the world to face. I remember one of my sons' elementary school teachers telling me that the first year of school and the seventh grade are often the most difficult for children because they are transitioning from one life situation— daycare or home in the former case, and elementary school in the latter—to the next. I believe that rule holds true our entire lives. We master one stage of life—caring for small children, let's say—and we achieve a certain degree of ease and calm. Our coping skills match the task at hand. We are unconsciously competent; we don't have to think about what we're doing because we have the skill to do it. Indeed, learning to master one life stage is quite like learning to master driving a manual-shift car: difficult at first, as you concentrate hard on remembering what to do and on doing it at the same time. But with practice, it becomes easier, and then one day you get into the driver's seat and arrive at your destination an hour later, and it was no effort at all to get there.

Change—transition to a new stage of life—is like learning a

whole new skill. The skills and habits we used to get us through the earlier stages of adulthood are not enough to get us through our later years. Our bodies aren't the same: we tire more easily, our metabolisms change. Our minds are different: the words don't always come so readily, and we can't recall details as quickly as we once did. The transition to older adulthood pushes us, once again, into the realm of "conscious incompetence." That's the stage of learning where you *know* you haven't got a firm hold on the skills you need. Our old ways of doing things no longer work.

In my case, I began to see that my life as I had organized it over the past fifteen years could not sustain me through the next twenty. I recognized that I must consciously change my ways— reorganize my life—in order to live as vibrantly and freely as possible. I spoke to friends and acquaintances about aging, and their feelings about the approach of older adulthood. A single theme bubbled up over and over: the need to prepare. I'm not talking about preparing in the Girl Scouts sense—making a list and checking it twice. Rather, the preparation we do in our fifties or sixties, depending on how early we start, touches every aspect of our lives: our finances, our health, our relationships, our beliefs, our work. Everything.

Simply put, women should prepare in their fifties for the rest of their lives. What we do today will affect how long we live, how healthy we will be, where we will live, how much fun we will have, how solvent we will be. The foundation for the rest of our lives is built on the choices we make and the actions we take in midlife.

If this sounds like hard work, it is. But the effort of consciously figuring out what sort of life you want to lead—and how you will make it happen—is also rewarding, fun and life-giving. Over the last decade, I have had the privilege of travelling across the country, giving hundreds of talks to tens of thousands of people. These presentations have usually focused on my journey through mental illness, but my audiences and the organizations that hire me are often not there to hear only about my life with bipolar disorder. They are there to hear me tell the story of my whole life. The high highs and the low lows. Pierre Trudeau. The Rolling Stones. I am an ordinary person, but I have been both blessed and cursed with an extraordinary life. When I speak, I share my experiences—and the hard-earned lessons I have learned. Someone once told me that I have a reputation for dangerous candour, and I suppose they are right.

When I finish my talk, I always make time to greet people from the audience, and I'm constantly surprised by the number of people—often women—who wait to speak to me. It makes me feel a bit shy; the insecure teenager inside me wonders why on earth they want to talk to *me*. But then these women begin sharing their stories with me, and my insecurity vanishes, replaced with a sense of gratitude and honour that I am able to bear witness to the experiences of others.

I often hear stories about people's experiences with mental illness. But more and more, women confide in me their thoughts, feelings, excitement and concerns about getting older. Our youth-oriented society does not have a clearly defined place for the older woman. Across this country, so many women tell me they want to live purposeful, meaningful lives throughout older adulthood. They just aren't always sure how.

Another thing these women tell me is that, even as they navigate the trials of aging, they are excited about getting older. There is a deep freedom in age that we simply don't experience as younger adults. We had to put everything aside for so long to raise our children, to work, to cut the grass and pay the bills on time, to build up our lives. But as we move north of 50, we enter a stage of life that has the potential to give us perfect freedom. We have the chance to finally live free of the constraints and responsibilities that shaped our younger lives. And because we are living longer than ever, that freedom has the potential to last for two, three or even four good decades.

But to truly relish the freedom this stage of life offers, we must prepare ourselves. Because the perils of old age—poverty, poor health, social isolation, boredom and hopelessness—are very real and closely connected to one another. Most worryingly, they can happen to us more easily than you might think. One day you are living a comfortable life; then something happens, and life as you know it has changed irrevocably.

Believe me, I know. I have seen the best and worst of what life has to offer. I have danced in the arms of presidents, dressed in haute couture, and I have been confined in a psychiatric institution, my bank account—and life—in shambles. I have ridden a motorcycle through the desert, clinging to a king for all I was worth, and I have attended AA meetings with the unemployed and homeless. I have met the pope on the shores of Lake Como, and I have held back tears, sitting on a dirt floor in a straw hut that serves as a classroom to dozens of malnourished children. Change is the order of life, and I have experienced this natural law as vividly as anyone.

You never, ever know when something life-changing is about to happen. And when it does, all you can count upon is the inner strength you have cultivated, and the systems and supports that exist in your life to help you through. I have met tremendous life challenges both prepared and unprepared. And I can tell you that being prepared is much, much better.

So how does one prepare to live a rich and vibrant older age? I always start by turning inward. One of the symptoms of bipolar disorder that I have experienced is a tendency toward racing ideas—my mind becomes a tangle of alternately sparkling and dark half-finished thoughts, each zinging through my head at a million miles a second. I have learned to breathe deeply, slow down and think methodically. In a life characterized by external change, I have learned that I am my own best starting point. I have to take the time to be alone, to know my own heart and articulate what it is that I truly want. Because life is such an epic journey, I have learned to break it down, piece by piece, examining the pillars of a well-lived life and questioning whether each of these pillars is strong enough to see me through the next thirty years.

For me, life and purpose are intricately connected. But our purpose changes as we grow older, as does the way in which we can contribute to the world. Adventure—a hallmark of my younger years—takes on a different nuance as we age. We have more time for adventure, but we can also become so addicted to comfort that we fail to remember the life-enhancing benefits of a good shake-up. Friendships, relationships, romance—these are really the underpinnings of a well-lived life. For instance, did you know that social isolation is considered as dangerous to our health as smoking? And speaking of smoking, our physical health in older adulthood underpins our ability to live well. Without our health, we really do have very little. Brain health and mental wellness are incredibly important aspects to consider, as are finances, and where and how we live. As we age we must also prepare ourselves for the inevitability of grief. Last, but not least, as we move into the rest of our lives, it is incumbent upon us to celebrate and honour the time, people and places we cherish.

We are moving into the exciting last stretches, you and I. We are getting closer to the peak of our adventure here on earth. There's still plenty of track ahead of us, and the going promises to be exhilarating, challenging and rewarding. Let's make the best of it.

Chapter 2

FIGURE OUT YOUR WHY

Rediscover your purpose.

In the late 1990s, I lost my son Michel in a skiing accident and then my first husband, Pierre, to cancer. An unbearable grief, combined with my bipolar illness, triggered a profound emotional and psychological breakdown. In a life full of ups and downs, this was my darkest hour. Appropriate medication and an intensive three-year period of psychotherapy and counselling helped me regain my psychological and neurological balance. But the key to moving from a place of mere existence to a place of true recovery was finding purpose.

In my case, it started with a job at Dada Destination Services in Ottawa, where I helped newcomers adjust to their lives in the city. Assisting newcomers with figuring out where to live, how to register for school or how to find a family doctor proved immensely rehabilitating to me. Through serving others, I was able to reconnect to a sense of meaning, contentment, hope and independence. The experience has deeply informed how I approach this next stage of my life. I know that finding new ways to serve others, indulging my interests and using my skills and insights, is an absolutely critical component of living—and aging—well.

Purpose gives our lives shape and meaning. Studies of older adults, such as one from the Rush University Medical Center, have found that having purpose later in life can contribute to a range of benefits, including better mental and physical health, higher everyday competence and socioeconomic status, and even being employed or having a meaningful romantic relationship. On the other hand, a lack of life purpose can lead to boredom, hopelessness, depression and, in extreme cases, even the loss of will to live. Indeed, I have learned first-hand how a sense of purpose contributes mightily to independence, hope and happiness.

Interestingly, studies have shown that men and women can approach finding purpose later in life quite differently, says Dr. Amy D'Aprix, a social worker and gerontologist who specializes in working with older women. Deep into middle age and older adulthood, Dr. D'Aprix says, "Women are still talking about what they want to create and do, whereas men are more often talking about how they want to kick back and relax." One major reason for this is that many women in their sixties spent large chunks of their lives out of the workforce, devoting their energies to caring for their families. As their children grow up and become independent, many women see older age as a time to pursue their interests and make an impact. Meanwhile, men—most of whom have worked their entire lives—may well be looking to relax on the greens.

But despite the fact that so many women are still looking to create and contribute throughout middle and older age, a number of factors can obscure our ability to find and live out our purpose as we get older. Retirement or the loss of a life partner can deprive a woman not only of her immediate sense of purpose, but also of the friends and social supports that may help her find a new purpose. Chronic illness, disability or declining health and cognitive function can make it harder for women to pursue their work, passions or volunteer activities. In some cultures, like Uganda's, for instance, it's common for grandparents to play a significant role in the day-to-day business of raising their grandchildren. But sociologists suggest that in our culture, there is a lack of clearly defined roles and opportunities for older adults to contribute their skills and wisdom. And finally, ageism can present a tremendous obstacle to older adults living out their purpose.

Vicky devoted her forty-year career to fundraising and alumni relations at a small college. The campus was her second home and she considered the students and alumni to be her extended family. She loved her work and derived a tremendous amount of personal satisfaction from her career. Then the board hired a new president. One of his first moves was to restructure operations in a way that ultimately eliminated Vicky's job. The president offered not-so-subtle hints that, given the rapid pace of change and the newly restructured environment, it might be a good idea for her to consider early retirement. Do you catch a whiff of ageism? Vicky did. Determined that no one would push her out of a job that had defined her, she dug her heels in and resolved to hang on until *she* decided she was going to retire.

Part of me admires Vicky's spunk and fire. Ageism is real, and across North America, many older women face acute challenges in finding or retaining meaningful work because of stereotypes about older workers—we're not up-to-speed with technology, we have too few working years left, we're slow and inefficient. A 2012 survey conducted for Revera suggests that almost two-thirds of Canadians over age 66 have been treated poorly because of their age, while 35 percent of all Canadians say they have treated someone differently because of their age. Meanwhile, a 2012 report called *Age-Friendly Workplaces*, produced by the federal, provincial and territorial ministers for seniors, outlines a broad range of benefits to hiring older workers. By 2036, one in four Canadians will be over 65, wreaking havoc on the workforce if companies refuse to hire older adults. In addition, older workers tend to be mature, productive and have a strong work ethic. We tend to have large social networks, and we often hold deep company knowledge or industry expertise, which we can pass on to a new generation of recruits. Despite these strengths, I continue to hear many experiences similar to Vicky's: smart, experienced and capable women getting edged out or turned down because of their age.

Employment lawyer Donna Ballman outlined, in a 2013 article for *Forbes*, numerous sneaky ways companies get rid of older workers. These include job elimination, layoffs, sudden downgrades in performance reviews (especially notable if you've had a history of solid reviews), threatening a person's pension, early retirement, cutting job duties, exclusion and isolation, denying opportunities for advancement, cutting hours and, in some extreme cases, even harassment. This is nothing short of disgusting. If you suspect you've been the victim of ageism, Ballman offers sage advice—keep track of the dates, location or any witnesses to age discrimination. Collect any documentation that supports your claim. For instance, if you notice that the best opportunities are going to younger workers, gather the documents you need to prove it. Keep your evidence at home and report your experience, using your company's policy and channel for reporting harassment.

As a large and influential group, we baby boomers have the power, clout and responsibility to knock ageism back, through advocacy and awareness building. And yet, what is sound advice for a group can be detrimental to the individual. In Vicky's case, she has resolved to stand up for her rights and show up at a workplace where she is no longer valued in order to fight the good fight. I ask: at what personal cost? Change is the order of life. Is Vicky fighting for her job, or for a reality that has long since changed? Our generation is no stranger to protest and peaceful demonstration. My view is that collectively we need to denounce ageism, openly discuss the challenges and opportunities surrounding older individuals and the workforce, and advocate for more support for older workers. At the same time, I believe that for every situation where contributions aren't valued, there are dozens more where they are prized. And this is where I believe we should be devoting our wisdom, competence and energy.

No matter what door we enter from, it seems that as we move through our sixth decade, many of us arrive at the thrilling yet uncomfortable chasm between the work that once defined us and the purpose we have yet to define. Transition times—whether we are entering seventh grade or our seventh decade, are challenging.

Dr. D'Aprix calls older adulthood "a pivotal time for women—almost like an identity crisis that you might commonly see in someone younger." As the old identities fall away, Dr. D'Aprix says, it's common for women to feel afraid, uncomfortable, or even to experience a period of depression as they struggle to fill the void with new purpose. "Women will often tell me, 'I don't think I'm done contributing, but I am probably done with what I just did.'" The problem, in many cases, is that they may not be sure what to do next. Turning inward is a crucial first step. The beauty of aging is that it offers a built-in tool for achieving the sense of quiet we need in order to truly turn inward and reflect: I'm speaking about the benefits of becoming invisible.

Embrace the Freedom of Invisibility

There was a time in my life when I was famous. For months after I separated from Pierre, photographers followed me around, snapping photos as I left hotels and restaurants, spinning overblown stories from the fragments of my life they witnessed. I learned that fame is a funny thing—it's both addictive and repulsive. Addictive because there is a part of the mind—the weak, insecure part—that exults in the attention. As human beings, we want to matter. So the flimsy, far-reaching haze of notoriety and celebrity can fool us into thinking that we are loved and valued by many. But the surge of energy that comes from being widely recognized can never make up for the prison that fame creates. I became repulsed by my surging narcissism and ego, fuelled by media attention. I had lost my footing.

I think of my old life when I observe today's celebrity culture, and the way our twenty-four-hour news cycle uses people one day and destroys them the next. At the height of my fame, I craved anonymity. After I left Pierre I was an aspiring photographer and got the great opportunity to spend a day apprenticing with the iconic photographer Richard Avedon in his New York studio. There was a horde of paparazzi outside, and we listened to them through the intercom and heard a distinctly British voice question whether there was a bedroom inside the studio that Richard and I might be using. What I wanted more than anything at that time was to walk around freely, invisible to everyone but myself.

Then I entered my sixties and I was suddenly reminded of the old adage about being careful what you wish for.

I am still a well-known person and as a speaker I can draw a crowd. But my days of paparazzi fame are long behind me. I am no longer the fresh-faced first lady of Canada. I melt into crowds in a way I never used to. When I walk into a room, I don't command interest the way I once did. Few people stop me on the street. I was once on a bus on my way home in Ottawa, unnoticed by all, when I heard a young man tell the bus driver that he was going to visit a friend whose apartment looked right onto Margaret Trudeau's balcony. (Yikes! I have learned one very valuable lesson in my life: privacy is the greatest luxury of all.) Forty years after I hid my face from the flashing bulbs and craved a cloak that would make me disappear, I finally got my wish. I am invisible.

Unless you have a high-powered position, the great disappearing act begins for most women in their fifties. A 2014 survey commissioned by A. Vogel, a natural herbal remedies company, suggests that by age 51, more than two-thirds of us feel completely unnoticed by the opposite sex. Our beauty and allure fades. For the most part, this doesn't bother me much. When I wake up in the morning and look in the mirror, I might notice a new line or wrinkle on my face. Part of me willingly accepts this as a feature of the aging process. But in a culture where attractiveness counts for so much, the loss of our beauty can make women feel that they are no longer important or worthy.

In a 2013 interview, the British actress Kristin Scott Thomas confided her fears that she would "disappear" into middle age. She said she felt "invisible," like an "old ragbag" when she walked the red carpet with younger actresses at the Cannes Film Festival. I ask you: if this is how Scott Thomas feels, what hope is there for the rest of us? Indeed, the same A. Vogel study reported that only 15 percent of women over age 51 reported high levels of confidence.

For me, the disappearing act was subtle yet profound. People still treat me kindly, but perhaps a little less courteously than they once did. I see my own disappearance in the person who politely holds the door open, but doesn't look me in the eye. A gaze might travel right past me, where once it lingered. A friend recently told me about the horror she felt when, in the eyes of a man who had given her a passing glance, she saw disinterest and even disappointment. After years of being noticed, I at first felt this lack of interest acutely. It angered me. I was still the same person, for pete's sake. At a party, I could still hold up my end of a spirited conversation. Why didn't people *see* me any longer?

It all could have been so different if I had had a brilliant career. Think: prime minister versus prime minister's plus-one.

The women in those positions who haven't shrunk into invisibility in middle age tend to be those who have pursued a high-powered career and are still working. Hillary Clinton comes to mind. These lifelong career women, like many of their male counterparts, have maintained their visibility by being powerful. That's why men don't fade away to the same degree that women do—they haven't dropped out of the workforce to raise children, or taken a low-profile job in order to have the flexibility women of our generation needed to balance the demands of family life.

But these choices that I, and so many others, made may compound the feeling of invisibility later in life. We lack professional networks and connections. The children who demanded our attention and nurturing grow up and learn to look after themselves. Those of us who did have a career retire, and the people who once looked to us for leadership are now running the show and making their own independent decisions. The hubbub of attention and activity that once nourished, enriched and complicated our lives begins to diminish. And all that is left is . . . ourselves.

When the great disappearing act first happened to me, I felt horribly invisible and disappointed. In my flower child days, I might have tried to organize a protest. Or at least a peaceful demonstration. But I am wiser and have less energy than I once did. I don't want to spend the next decade battling deeply held cultural beliefs. I want to enjoy myself. And so, I decided that if I had any hope of truly relishing my third act, I would have to find the upside of being invisible.

Embrace Who You Are

Life is a continuous process of rebuilding and reinvention. We take the lessons we have learned during one stage of life and apply them to the very different challenges of the next stage. In order to be successful, we have to confront the realities of our new life situation head-on. We must be open-minded and forward-looking. While I am encouraged by the growing awareness and debate surrounding ageist stereotypes in the world of work, in conversations with men and women my age about what it means to be older, I frequently encounter deep, internal fears about aging. In fact, one of the things I noticed while researching this book is the depth of stigma that exists within our culture, and our own hearts, about what it means to get older.

Dr. Martha Beck, a Harvard-educated sociologist and life coach and columnist for *O, The Oprah Magazine*, once conducted an experiment in a college class she was teaching. She asked her students to tear a piece of paper into multiple strips. On each strip, the students were instructed to write down something they loved—playing tennis, going to the beach, etc. Then she asked each of them to write down a reality of aging on a separate strip of paper. Much of what the students wrote down was negative— wrinkles, incontinence, using a cane. During the ensuing group discussion, she listened as many students expressed terror and disgust about the aging process. Next, Dr. Beck visited each desk and substituted one of the "Things I love to do" strips for the "Getting older" strip, to reframe the way the students perceived life in later years. "Our culture sees aging as devastating and horrible. We don't have space for the kinds of deep wisdom that age brings with it," says Dr. Beck.

Of course, this terror isn't limited to the young. I routinely encounter people who go to extraordinary lengths to stave off the reality of age, whether through surgery or expensive purchases of the sports car variety. It's easy to snicker when see what we believe to be a vain attempt to reclaim a vanished youth, but can we blame those people given the prevalence of ageism in our culture?

It wasn't always this way. For centuries, older adults were widely esteemed for their knowledge and experience, and thus held positions of power, authority and influence in their communities. Historians suggest that the invention of the printing press and the resulting rise of literacy robbed older adults of their social standing—books and pamphlets meant that older adults were no longer the sole repository of information. A century later, William Shakespeare thoughtfully enshrined the image of the shrunken, infirm elder in the "seven ages of man" monologue for *As You Like It*. The Industrial Revolution provided the final nail in the coffin. This great technological shift spurred families to be more mobile and adaptable in order to respond more quickly to market fluctuations. In an effort to boost their mobility, many families began looking for ways to cast off their older, far less mobile relatives, as outlined in *Disability and Aging Discrimination*, edited by Richard Wiener and Steven Wilborn.

Today, our society is terrified of age. As Dr. Beck's exercise models, when we think of getting older, what many of us see are the wonderful things we might no longer do, and the dreadful things we have to anticipate. One study into aging has found that many people—young and old—think it's all downhill after 50. A 2010 *Economist* article called "The U-Bend of Life" reported that researchers at Duke University surveyed a group of 30-year-olds and a group of 70-year-olds about which cohort they believed was happier. Both said the 30-year-olds were happier. But in fact, when asked to rate their well-being, the septuagenarians were the happier group. *The Economist* notes that other studies have shown that all the negative emotions—worry, anger, sadness and stress—decline as we get older.

Now that I am, technically speaking, a senior citizen, I too have found that the stigma doesn't fit the experience. Yes, it's true, I have replaced downhill skiing with yoga. But I have also replaced naiveté with the wisdom of the mature mind. Youthful insecurity has been edged out by the freedom and power that come when no one is watching.

Women of my generation grew up facing many social rules about who, what and how we should be. But to embrace the possibilities of this next phase of our lives, we must forget the stereotype that being old and invisible is the beginning of the end for a woman. Years of intensive therapy have taught me to question ruthlessly the belief that underpins any depressive thought. What if getting older is the beginning of something not only new but *better*?

In her wonderful memoir *My Life So Far*, Jane Fonda likens life after 60 to the third act of a play—the part where we bring together the various threads of our lives in order to make a meaningful contribution. For some people, this meaningful contribution is working with the poor. For others, it's deepening relationships with friends and family. And for others, it's finally pursuing the passions they might have delayed while raising children. There are so many options available to us: volunteering, pursuing a career or business, travelling, spending time with family, taking up an interesting hobby. With so many options it can be overwhelming to figure out what to do. In such cases, I have found it is often helpful to slow down, check in and listen to the silence.

I always admired Pierre for his tremendous ability to be silent. When he was prime minister, he would often come home and complain not about the stress, but about the noise—he was a man who needed peace and solitude. He found his silence through prayer and long walks through nature. He taught me to embrace solitude as well. On Saturday afternoons, he would often take the boys so I could have time for myself. I'd pack a picnic lunch, get into the car and drive to some secluded place where I'd sit back and listen to CBC's *Saturday Afternoon at the Opera*. It was a wonderful, life-enriching experience—an oasis of quiet in an otherwise frenetic world.

Learn to Just Be

My son Kyle called me recently and asked me what I would be doing that day. I looked around the gentle clutter of my apartment and tried to remember if I had any appointments. I didn't.

As a speaker and advocate for mental health, I go through intense periods when I criss-cross the country giving dozens of talks. I also have periods when my schedule slows down and I have much more time to sit quietly and simply think. Some women, especially those who have led busy lives, rail against the inevitable periods of quiet that older adulthood can offer. Yet during these quiet, uneventful hours, something useful, profound and meaningful may be afoot. After I spent so many years being far too much in the limelight, the life I have built for myself is a good balance between being out there and being private and solitary. A doctor at a cocktail party once said I was an "ambivert: sometimes extraverted, sometimes introverted." I try my hardest not to completely retreat into my own world, but the temptation is always there. One has to make oneself seen and heard from time to time. I do spend a lot of time in my mind.

Nancy retired seven years ago from a job she loved. She was a top financial analyst, frequently interviewed on TV and widely considered to be an expert in consumer products and retail trends. She was the quintessential working mom. She raised five children with her husband, didn't take maternity leaves, worked long hours and spent her evenings and weekends with her family. She didn't want to retire from her job. But then her employer denied her a two-week leave to help her aging mother. So Nancy quit and was abruptly and prematurely thrust into the world of retirement.

At first her pace of life didn't change. Her children were still in high school and university and needed her more than ever. She took over the gardening and cooking duties she'd once delegated to others. She served on a number of corporate and charity boards. But five years into retirement, Nancy's life began to change. Her board terms wound down. Her children got older and moved away. She remembered that she actually disliked cooking and gardening. She realized, with the exception of spending more time with her children and serving on boards, that she'd spent the last five years doing a lot of things she didn't necessarily enjoy. So the question was, what to do next? "For women, the natural progression is to stay busy," Nancy says. "But you could fill the day with activities and never take a moment to think, 'Does any of this stuff actually make me happy?'"

In Nancy's case, serendipity intervened. Her daughter was attending a cordon bleu cooking school in Paris and invited Nancy to come and share her apartment for three months. Nancy's first reaction was a firm no—she couldn't possibly leave her husband and life in Vancouver for that long, she told herself. Her husband encouraged her to reconsider. "Three months with your 22-year-old daughter in Paris," he pointed out. "How often does that happen?" Then she remembered a piece of advice her late father had given her. He had died alone on his sailboat after a week-long solo sailing expedition. Sailing had been his great passion, and he often went out to sea on his own. "You need to know what makes you happy," he told Nancy. "And you have to be willing to go it alone." But, she wondered, what exactly *would* she "go alone"?

The job Nancy had retired from—working as a financial analyst—saw her out the door most days by 3:30 a.m. and home fourteen hours later. Evenings were consumed taking the children to various activities. She'd spent her entire adult life in demand. Time had always been a scarce resource and now suddenly it was plentiful. If she was going to have any hope of truly savouring retirement, she realized, she'd need to figure out what made her happy. So she went to Paris.

Her daughter left early each morning and spent most of the day at school, so Nancy had endless hours to herself. One quiet, relaxed day stretched into another. "I began to remember how to just *be*," she says. She woke in the mornings and watched the sun slide across the ceiling. She took her time over breakfast. She people-watched and reacquainted herself with the things she loved to do—visiting galleries, touring museums, going to concerts. And in that calm, unhurried place, she found a sense of happiness and freedom that was totally unique in her hectic life.

Many of the women interviewed for this book reported that their younger years were often coloured with an uncomfortable urgency, a sense of striving. But while their uncomfortable urgency diminished with age, their desire for purpose and meaning increased.

In her work with countless women, Dr. Beck has witnessed the same thing. As we age and the reality of our mortality draws a shade closer, we begin to look for the deeper meaning of life, and in so doing, we feel greater amounts of peace, equanimity, comfort, "and all the things that help you experience greater depths of understanding, goodness, gladness and happiness." This peace is perhaps at the root of the advice so many of my friends say they would give their younger selves: *Don't fret so much. Just be.*

After I got off the phone with Kyle that day, I sat down at my dining room table with a cup of coffee. I sipped it quietly and stroked my cat, Aurora. I was happy to just be. That was my Paris. I encourage all women to find theirs.

Use Your Inner Compass
Learning to appreciate solitude and our own company is a prerequisite for the appearance of what Dr. Beck calls the "inner com-

pass." This compass is the wise, intuitive voice inside that reminds us who we are and what is most important to us. As Nancy describes it, tuning into this inner compass is essential to fulfillment in our third act. "Finding out what makes you happy and knowing what makes you unhappy is an important part of the process."

After studying why older people—women especially—tend to get happier as they age, Stanford University psychology professor Laura Carstensen told a reporter from *The Economist* about the "uniquely human ability to recognize our mortality and monitor our own time horizons." In other words, the closer we get to death, the better we understand what matters most. I think of it as a new phase of the biological clock.

Think about it for a second. How many hundreds of hours did you spend as a young woman doing things you didn't really enjoy doing? A glamorous, straight-talking friend of mine, Dotty, now refuses to spend a single minute at a social engagement she doesn't love. Gone are the days of staying put out of a sense of politeness. "The moment I'm tired, I'm gone," she says.

Dr. Beck suggests that older women are perhaps the most skilled at finding—and listening to—our inner compass. And when we do, the rewards are evident not only for ourselves, but for the people we serve.

Find Purpose through Meaningful Work

Annette Verschuren's inner compass sprang loudly to life after her fiftieth birthday. A legend in corporate Canada, Annette was a Cape Breton farm girl turned CEO who, among other things, led Home Depot's expansion from a handful of stores in the 1990s to close to two hundred today. Throughout her career, Annette was driven by the sense of achievement and competitiveness that drives so many CEOs. But she noticed after she turned 50 that she had a longing to explore the entrepreneurial side of herself—the part of her that didn't want to report to a board, but wanted instead to run her own business. "I was intensely curious, but I had limitations. I had people I had to report to."

So in 2012 she launched her own energy storage company, NRStor Inc. The firm is on the cutting edge of providing reliable energy storage that can reduce our dependence on fossil fuels. Getting this important venture off the ground required the total sum of her experiences at the helm of corporations. And while she still has to report to her investors, Annette has much more freedom now than she ever did before. In claiming this freedom, she has uncovered a profound sense of joy and purpose. "This is the happiest time of my life. And . . . I can honestly say that it's because I'm doing what I love and I don't care what people think of me."

In fact, studies reported by *The Economist* suggest that happiness traces a U-shaped curve as we age. We begin our adult lives relatively cheerful, but the social pressures of living—earning money, raising families, striving in our careers—cause our happiness to decline throughout our thirties, forties and even early fifties. Life is rich with meaning during those years, but it is also a stressful and sometimes unhappy experience. By middle age, however, especially for women who are financially secure (many aren't), those pressures lift and happiness increases throughout the later decades of our lives.

By our sixties, we know and accept who we are, and this

brings inordinate peace and freedom. Like me, Annette spent much of her adulthood trying to figure out and become the person she was. "I'm finally there. It's the weirdest feeling in the world, but it's so much fun." Settling into your own skin and finding the freedom that comes from knowing who you are brings not only a sense of fun, but also a peace of mind that can be exhilarating.

Knowing who you are and understanding how your body of work and experience can empower and serve others was another important theme I noticed among the women interviewed who are making a difference in their later years.

Marg Hachey discovered her love of business in her late twenties. After her youngest son started school, she found a job selling cosmetics for Avon and soon worked her way into a management position. A few successful years later, she became partner in Duocom, a Montreal-based company that sold audiovisual equipment. Over the next twenty years, Marg and her business partner built the company from $2 million in sales to $50 million. In the late 1990s, she sold the company to an international conglomerate—which managed to bankrupt Duocom in just a few short years. Desperate to save the company she'd sacrificed so much to build, not to mention the jobs of hundreds of employees, some of whom had worked for her most of their careers, Marg scrambled to get the cash she needed to re-purchase the assets of the company and save it. She did so, rebuilt the firm and then sold it—for the last time—in 2010.

After she "retired" from running a multi-million dollar business, Marg faced the same existential challenge so many of us do— now what? I know many type-A business people who leave the cutthroat corporate world only to indulge their inner competitors on, say, the golf course. Marg chose differently. Her thirty-year career as an entrepreneur taught her some powerful and hard-won lessons about what it takes to grow a business and maintain a semblance of harmony at home. In her sixties, she didn't want to build up another huge business, but she was still fascinated by businesses and by the women who ran them. She began using her own experiences and insights to coach a new generation of women entrepreneurs. But as Marg attended networking events, she discovered that there were many women who needed her advice but couldn't afford to pay her coaching fees. So together with a friend, she co-founded GroYourBiz, a national network of personal advisory boards that provides support and mentorship to women entrepreneurs. And while sharing her experience and knowledge has been tremendously gratifying, it has also given her a great deal of enjoyment. "I go to a conference and it is major shopping, major wine, major learning and camaraderie." In the business world, Marg was so often the lone woman. By founding an advisory network for women entrepreneurs, "it was like we built the old girls' club, finally."

Marg's story is a terrific example of how we can use our enduring passion—in her case, growing businesses—as a guide to help us uncover a new sense of purpose. But her story also points out an important role we can play in the lives of younger women: that of mentor. Mentoring is an excellent way to leverage our passion for our careers and the lessons we've learned along the way. It allows us to stay connected with work we love but may no longer wish to do every day.

In a 2011 article on "female mid-life crisis" for *Psychology*

Today, executive coach Marcia Reynolds describes the challenge faced by many successful career women in mid- and later life—a "restless craving to realize their potential," often outside the career they have built for themselves. Reynolds suggests the source of this identity struggle isn't that they don't know who they are, but rather, that they seek a new, deeply meaningful way to "apply their greatness." In Marg's case, she chose to "apply her greatness" to women trying to achieve the same aspirations she herself had achieved.

Finding ways to share our skills and wisdom for the betterment of others is one significant way to find meaning in older age. More and more women are doing this and thereby flipping the stereotype that equates aging to a loss of power. There are countless examples of women for whom age has only reinforced their desire to have an impact and their ability to be a positive influence.

I feel my sense of purpose renewed each time I visit my grandchildren. When I first held little Pierre, my first grandchild, I felt a whole new passion to make the world a better place for him—this little baby who had so much of Sacha and Zoë in him but also Pierre and me. My grandchildren renew within me a commitment to use my current freedom to make a positive difference.

The question of how to elevate the world's most desperately poor citizens has bedevilled governments and NGOs for decades. For two decades, Swedish national Ingrid Munro worked with people living in abject poverty as the head of the African Housing Fund, which served the homeless, including many who lived in the slums of Nairobi. In 1988, Ingrid and her Canadian husband befriended a seven-year-old boy from the slums. They later adopted him and his two brothers. Through the boys, Ingrid heard countless stories of homeless slum women who looked after them, providing them with what little food or shelter they could manage. After Ingrid retired, **the beggars** she'd formerly worked with routinely visited her house, **pleading** that she not abandon them.

She decided to help them, with one caveat: that they help themselves first. She told them that for every shilling they saved, she would lend them two. In 1999, she began offering $5 loans to a group of fifty beggar women. She named the organization Jamii Bora, which in Swahili means "good families." Today, the Jamii Bora Bank is the largest microfinance institution in Kenya, claiming more than 300,000 members. A year into the venture, Ingrid discovered that the clients most commonly defaulted on loans when a family member became ill and they had to make the difficult choice between paying medical bills and repaying their loan. No standard insurer would cover her members, so Ingrid decided to do it herself. She started by offering insurance to members for $12 per year—which covered the adult member and up to four children, with additional children costing a couple extra dollars. Insurance is even offered to people living with HIV and AIDS. As of 2006, the insurance arm covered its costs through premiums, and not a dollar of donor money was used to pay for claims.

While many of the world's NGOs, governments and poverty experts argue over whether the world's poorest can actually handle microfinance (many believe these people first require a safety net before they can take on a micro loan), Ingrid and the fifty beggar women who founded Jamii Bora with her have quietly gone about the business of elevating thousands of people above poverty. A 2012 video by Results Educational Fund features one of the original beggars, Joyce Wairimu, who parlayed her initial $5 loan into six small businesses with sixty-two employees.

Find Purpose through Volunteerism

I've known Dotty for most of my life. We grew up across the street from each other in North Vancouver and our two families had an open-door policy. One of the Sinclair girls was always at the Meyers' residence and vice versa. Dotty and I shared similar personalities—outgoing, and with a joy for life. We always felt more like sisters than friends.

As a young woman, Dotty ran a successful upscale clothing boutique. I modelled for her when she started out, and continued doing so even after I married Pierre. She was just always such fun to be around. Dotty has a straight-shooting wit that I adore. Her husband, Bud, was a successful restaurateur and Dotty helped him run the business. They lived in a spectacular West Vancouver waterfront home. One day Dotty came home from a shopping trip and carried her bags confidently past Bud, who was reading the newspaper. (I, on the other hand, would probably have tried to hide my shopping bags.)

"Dotty, I think you've got enough clothes, don't you?" he said.

Dotty put down her bags and marched over to her husband. "Bud," she declared. "I didn't marry you to be poor." Confidently putting words to things many of us would think but not say. That's Dotty.

Dotty and Bud sold their businesses a few years ago and that's

when Dotty threw herself into charity work. As a former restaurateur, she understood the importance of running a tight ship, cultivating relationships with people who would support her business,
and getting to know journalists to whom she could pitch news stories. As a fundraiser, first for a firefighters' organization, Dotty was
able to put these marketing and organizational skills to excellent
use. She created the first firefighters calendar the organization had
ever put out. The work had its benefits, she allowed, but "it's not as
glamorous as people think." She hustled all over the city, organizing
photo shoots, coordinating firefighter schedules and dealing with
graphic designers and printers. The calendars sold out each year.

Finding herself ready for a new challenge, she then turned
her attention to a Christian organization that provided housing
and support services for the homeless. The charity was suffering,
and Dotty saw an opportunity to fire things up. So she started
organizing a swimsuit fashion show as a fundraiser. The charity's
leadership didn't think her idea fit with their religious beliefs.
"I'm a Christian, and it fits with my beliefs" was Dotty's retort.
"And besides, Christians DO wear bathing suits." Dotty and the
bikini-hating charity soon parted ways.

Two years ago, however, Dotty stumbled upon an organization that needed her help badly. The Vancouver Native Health
Society was a small clinic that provided medical aid to Aboriginal women and their children. About half these women were
HIV positive. All the medical staff were volunteers. Each day
they fed two hundred people, and when Dotty did her first walk-
through, they were feeding all those people from just a couple
of hot plates. Dotty's tour guide cried as she moved through the

rundown building, explaining the severity of the need and their lack of resources. "You talk about pulling my heart string," Dotty later said. "It was phenomenal. I walked through those doors and I knew I was in the right place."

Dotty instantly got to work fundraising and organizing for a new kitchen to be installed. Any chance she got, she told all her friends about the Vancouver Native Health Society. One afternoon she was hiking with a wealthy friend in the mountains near Palm Desert, California, where she and Bud spend the winters.

"What do you need most help with?" her friend asked.

"We need a part-time nurse," Dotty said.

That afternoon her friend wrote a cheque to cover the wages of a part-time nurse for the centre.

Dotty spends much of her time in Palm Desert thinking about her next trip back to Vancouver. "This is my purpose in life," she says. "This is what I'm here for. I'm not just here to plan fun activities, I'm here to make a difference."

She meets people all the time who, seeing her passion and sense of duty, want to throw themselves into the world of volunteer work. Her advice: don't overcommit. Choose an organization that shares your worldview. For instance, I doubt Dotty will volunteer with organizations that believe bathing suits are un-Christian. Start with a small commitment—two hours, once a month. Build up slowly, once you truly understand what it is you're getting into. We have life experience and broad skills under our belts, but remember, at this stage of life, the quality of the energy we bring to our work is different. One might say that after 60, two hours is the new four hours.

Like Dotty, I have derived tremendous satisfaction from my volunteer work—in my case as director of several national organizations devoted to brain health and mental wellness, as well as charity work with WaterCan, now WaterAid Canada, a national charity devoted to fighting poverty by helping the world's poorest people gain access to clean water and basic sanitation. My work with WaterAid has given me an opportunity to travel to some of the world's poorest countries to witness first-hand the ravages of poverty, as well as the socioeconomic transformation that something as basic as a community well can create. I am able to put my identity as a public figure to use by advocating for clean water and basic sanitation for the world's poor, spreading awareness about the issue of desperate poverty and raising much-needed funds.

In fact, I believe my work for WaterAid is the very best work I do. In many parts of the world, women must walk great distances to get water, often risking their own safety in the process. Providing clean drinking water in their own village reduces child mortality, frees girls up to be educated and gives their mothers an opportunity to take on paying work. There is nothing more gratifying to me than to use my skills, influence and energy to help and empower other women. Indeed, if our world is to change, I believe women must stand side by side, helping each other to create lasting change and opportunities.

But my work with WaterAid isn't just about other people—it's about me. I know the pain of losing a child. And in Africa, I have met so many women who understand my pain. I want to make a difference, and I have found a simple way—delivering clean water and sanitation—that can prevent thousands of women from knowing the pain I experienced.

As important as my professional and volunteer work is to me, I derive just as much satisfaction and purpose from my role as a grandmother. My grandchildren are truly the passion of my life. I anticipate their weekend visits, relish the hours I spend with them and remember our raucous fun vividly after they have gone. Women can find satisfaction in a range of activities: attending exercise classes, babysitting grandchildren, learning a new language or playing chess, to name a few. Finding activities that you enjoy so much that you lose track of time is every bit as important as finding opportunities to serve others. In a balanced life, we have both.

In fact, understanding what you love to do is key to uncovering your purpose, says Stephen Cope, the founding executive director of the Kripalu Institute for Extraordinary Living and author of *The Great Work of Your Life: A Guide for the Journey to Your True Calling*. Cope advises people who feel stuck or uncertain about finding purpose to answer three questions: What fascinates you? What compels you? What challenges are you facing?

Cope argues that we get the most satisfaction out of life when we understand our purpose and truly live it. This is not about going through the motions, he says. You might be living your purpose and doing the work your life has prepared you to do, but if you aren't doing it *intentionally*, you won't feel as keenly the abiding sense of joy you get from living purposefully. In this, as in so many other things, Dolly Parton has some choice words. The key to happiness, she says, is to "figure out who you are and do it on purpose."

Personally, I am fascinated by the notion of regarding life's challenges as a source of purpose. This is especially poignant in older adulthood, as so many of us deal with declining health and loss.

A few years ago, a close friend of mine died of cancer. Toward the end of his life, his entire purpose seemed to be devoted to overcoming the challenges his illness brought upon him: dealing with pain, discomfort and the stark reality of impending death. I witness other friends whose purpose is deeply tied to caring for parents or partners who are dealing with other serious diseases. Witnessing their remarkable and often difficult journeys underscores the idea that sometimes we meet our purpose as we confront our challenges.

One of the biggest challenges of my life right now is facing the sometimes difficult realities of age, and figuring out how to make the time I have left as meaningful, useful and productive as possible. I live my purpose as I write this book; I live it in the conversations I engage in with my family and friends. The beauty of finding purpose is that it compels, intrigues and consumes. My family, my work, my volunteerism—all these things inspire and motivate me. These deeply purposeful activities awaken in me a sense of curiosity, of wonder.

Now, when I confront the challenges of being a woman in her mid-sixties—the feelings of invisibility or the potential of deteriorating health—I don't feel scared.

CHAPTER 3

MAKE FRIENDS WITH YOUR BUCKET LIST

Shake up your routine by pursuing the adventures
for which you now have time.

I have always loved adventure. Perhaps that's why downhill skiing has been a lifelong passion: the constant negotiation between speed and control, the cold air and bright snow, the panoramic views of wintry countryside. Skiing, as all good adventures do, challenges my complacence, encourages me to push limits and reminds me that I'm alive.

Because my life has been full of adventure, I've grown so accustomed to life's transformative properties that for a time I forgot about them. And then, in 2006, I was reminded all over again.

While married to Pierre, I had the opportunity to travel to the farthest corners of the world. I saw many incredible things, and I also bore witness to the abject poverty in which many millions of people live. This sparked within me a desire to do all I can to relieve this suffering. In 2005, my daughter-in-law Sophie Grégoire-Trudeau and I decided to travel to Ethiopia together, along with a camera crew and a team from WaterCan. While Sophie had travelled throughout her life, it would be the first time she would experience true poverty. Ethiopia is one of the world's most stunning countries, and one of the world's poorest. WaterCan estimates that 90 percent of rural Ethiopians live without access to clean water or basic sanitation.

Sophie and I travelled throughout the exquisite countryside, touring communities that had been transformed by the installation of life- and hope-giving wells and latrines. One day, after driving over kilometres of a rugged road that was more of a riverbed, we came to a remote village with a tiny school. The school was little more than a straw hut with dirt floors and a few benches. There were no books, papers, pencils or posters of any kind. The children met us at our trucks and pressed on us the whole time. We were the first white women they had seen.

I have always been sensitive to crowds and immediately felt uncomfortable. But I wanted desperately to show my support and so I stayed inside the hut as more and more children pressed in. It was a hot day and the air soon smelled strongly of little unwashed bodies. The children were joyous and smiling, but as a mother, I was cut deeply by the sight of them, so poor and malnourished. I began to have difficulty breathing. Beside me, Sophie—my elegant and sophisticated daughter-in-law—was telling stories, laughing, smiling and engaging with the children. I stayed as long as I could and then got up abruptly to leave. Sophie and the children carried on.

"I'm so sorry, Sophie," I told her later. "It was the sight of the poverty, the heat and the smell—I was overwhelmed."

"What smell?" she asked.

What you need to know about Sophie is that she has the most finely attuned nose of anyone I've met. She can pick out the perfume someone is wearing if they are in another room. But in the midst of our life-changing adventure and mission to Ethiopia, her mission completely overtook her. I was awed to see the transformation, and reminded of the power of venturing far beyond the world we know.

Seek Adventure in the Third Act

I thought that after a certain age I would lose my taste for adventure. But while I have grown to love the stability of my current life, I still yearn for the sweet discomfort of new experiences. And I am not alone in this. While the stereotype is that women slow down in older adulthood and seek no more adventure than the rhythm of a rocking chair, the reality is quite different, say psychologists, therapists and coaches who work with older women.

"At this stage of life, many women are looking for a change," says Resa Eisen, a Toronto-based therapist. "They've been married a million years. They've raised their children, been in careers, they've done their work. As they move into their sixties and seventies, they're saying, 'Now I want a change ... something out of the routine, something creative.' Some want to completely change their lives around. Others simply want to expand."

This desire for change and expansion manifests in different ways, says Eisen. Some women want to divorce their husbands and try life as a singleton. Some women's appetite for adventure may be sated by trying out new recipes or learning how to play an instrument. Others want to travel to distant corners of the world or take up extreme hobbies like pole dancing. Eisen has seen it all: when one of her clients showed up to a session one morning and announced she wanted to climb Mount Everest and then move permanently to a remote place in the developing world, she was amused, but hardly surprised.

So where does this newfound craving for adventure come from? Dr. Martha Beck says that for women in their third act, a number of interrelated forces are at work, all of which nudge us from the world in which we've grown comfortable into the realm of the unknown. The first and perhaps most significant of these drivers is a growing awareness of our own mortality.

Dr. Beck was 18 when, during a training run for an upcoming marathon, she was side-swiped by a passing car. She sustained minor injuries from the accident, and experienced bruises and aches in the immediate aftermath. Her doctor told her to rest until the pain went away. But the pain didn't go away. For the next twelve years, she battled severe and undiagnosed body pain that kept her in bed for weeks and sometimes months at a time. After being treated by dozens of specialists, Dr. Beck was ultimately diagnosed with fibromyalgia.

Despite facing one of the most trying experiences of her life, Dr. Beck, now 51, says that her illness also gave her a chance to think about and appreciate life. She was a young woman at the time, but such periods of reflection and gratitude brought on by failing health are something many older adults experience. In fact, Dr. Beck, who has coached thousands of clients, describes "life accident" phenomena—instances in which a major accident that threatens a person's health or survival brings about a sense of life-affirming gratitude. As we age, lose loved ones or experience new risks to our own health or survival, "aging becomes the life accident we run into. It starts awakening us." And the result of that awakening, says Dr. Beck, is often a quest for meaning, growth and adventure.

In Dr. Beck's case, after her fibromyalgia diagnosis and resulting return to health, she quit her job as a university professor teaching sociology and business management to start a new adventure as a life coach and writer. Adventures can, and often do, come in the form of a career change.

Betty's Mountain Top

Betty Steinhauer's brush with mortality led her on a very different type of quest. Her early life was marked by loss and trauma. She was raped at the age of 13. Two years later, her father died, leaving her alone with her mother, who suffered from schizophrenia. Betty was forced to quit school in Grade 9 so that she could earn money and take care of her mother. She was married by the time she was 20 and gave birth to two children. The challenges of her early life forged in Betty a steely determination to succeed, and a love of discipline and order.

She started a government relations consultancy, and worked with top CEOs and even prime ministers (including Pierre). She travelled all over the world—to 155 countries, in total—attending conferences and working with clients. She was successful, well-paid and a self-described control freak. "My life had to be controlled and organized 100 percent," she says.

Then, in her late sixties, Betty began to catch herself dreaming about giving up her business and her swanky Toronto life for a more nomadic existence. Something deep inside her wanted to travel, not because she had a conference or meeting to attend, but to experience life in a vastly different place. She ignored the voice. "I couldn't take it seriously, because the idea of giving up the life I had built in Toronto was very risky. I was afraid." Yet something in Betty rebelled against this fear. As she looked around at her cohorts, what she noticed was how many of them had become more "obsessed by rules" as they aged. She noticed social conventions, for instance, that older adults "should" take up golf or spend winters in Florida. "I saw people falling into a routine and forgetting about their passions because they were worried about what might happen. They stopped looking at the possibilities because they were too concerned about all the 'what ifs.'" Indeed, in her own life, Betty's "what ifs" were holding her back from travelling the world.

Then, she had the accident.

It happened a few months before her seventieth birthday. A car struck her, sending Betty to the hospital with non-life-threatening injuries. It took three months of intensive therapy with a personal trainer and chiropractor for Betty to "put herself back together." And while the accident wasn't life threatening, it was life changing.

"I realized—all of a sudden—that if I had any ideas about

things I wanted to do, now was the time to do them. If I was afraid, if I thought something was risky . . . I just told myself, 'Forget it, Betty, and just go ahead and do it.'"

And so, as assiduously as she had worked on her muscles, Betty now began working on her fear.

When it comes to pursuing growth, change and adventure, the power of fear can't be underestimated. Normally fear serves a useful purpose—it keeps us safe. For instance, when walking through a foreign city, Betty tunes into her fear, paying attention to her gut to figure out which streets are safe and which streets should be avoided. The trouble is when our fear becomes akin to twenty-four-hour news, blasting out horror stories at all hours. And indeed most of the time, fear works this way. To quote Mark Twain, "I've lived through some terrible things in my life, some of which actually happened."

In her book *Steering by Starlight*, Dr. Martha Beck describes the physical source of fear: a layer deep inside the brain—wrapped around the brain stem in fact—called the "reptilian brain," so named because it first developed in these early vertebrates. The purpose of this part of the brain is to keep us alive by transmitting what Dr. Beck calls "lack and attack fears." You may have experienced "lack fears" regarding money—perhaps you're concerned you don't have enough, or you fear you'll run out of it. "Attack fears" are worries that someone might invade your house, or that something terrible might befall you on the streets of Portugal—a country you just happen to want to visit during retirement. While some of these lack and attack fears make sense in the moment—say, Betty's instinct that a particular street in a foreign city is unsafe—if we don't learn to distinguish between rational and irrational fears, we may never pursue our dreams. Adventure nearly always pushes us out of our comfort zone. And our lizard brains adore the comfort zone.

Because our worries over what might happen are so often irrational, taking the time to carefully investigate our fear is an important step in overcoming it. In Betty's case, because she initially viewed her desire to leave her Toronto life and become a nomad as risky, she didn't fully explore the idea. After her accident, however, she began contemplating *why* she wanted to pursue this "risky" adventure. For starters, she had always loved to travel, and living abroad would give her plenty of opportunity to do that. At the age of 70, she had outlived both her parents. She had no siblings. Her children were both healthy and well-adjusted adults. "I realized I had nothing to lose by going."

Next, Betty began exploring her worst-case scenarios. Because she'd already done so much travelling in her life, she didn't have the safety fears that a first-time traveller might experience. She trusted in her own ability to keep herself safe. But she did worry about health insurance, and what might happen if she were to get sick. So she did some research and discovered that the Ontario Health Insurance Plan (OHIP), the public health insurance provider in the province of Ontario, allowed Ontario residents to take a one-time, two-year "sabbatical." All she had to do was fill out an application form—just this once—and OHIP would partially insure her overseas. Additional private insurance would cover the costs associated with flying her home if she were sick or injured seriously enough to warrant it.

Another major worry was that she had a lovely apartment filled with art, beautiful furniture and other assorted belongings. While she didn't mind giving up her apartment, she wasn't prepared to live without a true home base. She confided her fears in a good friend, who made Betty an offer she ultimately couldn't refuse. "She offered me a room in their home where I could keep my most valuable things and [that I could] use as a home base whenever I chose."

And Betty's final worry was failure—the fear of what she'd do if her big, travel-the-world-and-live-like-a-nomad plan didn't work out. This fear had kept her stuck for some time because "I had no idea what would happen if things didn't work out for me." So she forced herself to think through the fear, and what she would do. "I realized I'd come home to Toronto, rent another apartment, get my stuff out of storage, hang my art back on my walls and buy some new furniture from IKEA."

A surprising thing happened. "Things started clicking into place, without me having to exert much effort." She found an excellent and trustworthy bookkeeper to ensure her bills were paid and that her finances remained in order. Friends volunteered to keep pieces of art or furniture that couldn't go into storage. And as she planned her trips, beautiful, affordable accommodations fell into her lap. Some she found online, such as a lovely flat in the heart of Athens, while others were recommended to her by friends, such as a shared flat near Mallorca.

A few months after her seventieth birthday, Betty left for India, thus launching her nomadic adventure. From there she travelled to Switzerland, France, Scotland and Spain, with brief touchdowns in Toronto for visits with her children and four grandchildren. As a globe-trotting consultant, Betty had become a master networker, and by the time she retired from her business, she had four filled-to-the-rim Rolodexes. She has remained in touch with her contacts and visits them as she travels. She still attends conferences and lets her friends know where she's going next. By cultivating these relationships, she is often able to find local acquaintances to show her around. She's frequently invited by new or old friends to visit, and she does this, peppering her European sojourns with brief trips to, say, Arizona. Accepting invitations and saying yes to new friendships has deeply enriched her life, Betty says, and has the unexpected but bonus impact of reducing her costs even more. Overall, she is able to travel the world for the same monthly cost as living in Toronto, she says.

Along the way, she met a man who coined the term "nomadic intern" to describe Betty's lifestyle. Betty liked the phrase and started a blog of the same name where she details her adventures. Adventure has also opened up new possibilities for what's next in her life. "This was never a 'final hoorah,'" Betty says. "I've always viewed this nomadic existence as another adventure in my life—another phase." In the beginning, her primary goal was to learn and volunteer—to learn the language and customs of her host country, to experience the culture, and to give back by volunteering her time and expertise. Volunteering has given her a chance to meet interesting people and really settle into the local life while maintaining a deeper sense of purpose. For instance, after a newfound friend confided in Betty that she was trying to get a development centre for children off the ground in Spain—a country hit hard by the global recession—Betty put her government relations skills to work by helping the woman set up a board of directors in order to ensure the organization was sustainable and capable of attracting grants and other funding.

And in the midst of all this adventure, the next chapter of Betty's life is revealing itself—an innovative, invitation-only retirement community in a warm, welcoming country where older adults can come together, learn from each other and use their collective wisdom to creative positive and powerful social change. She's calling it Betty's Mountain Top.

While the reality of their own mortality may drive some women to seek adventure, there is another important force that comes into play deep in middle age: freedom. Some older adults will enter their sixties and seventies caring for their aging parents or spouses, but there are many—me, for instance—for whom this is a period of relative freedom. Our children are independent, our careers have perhaps slowed down and, for the first time in our adult lives, our time is our own, should we choose to claim it.

Arlene's Children's Village

Arlene Brown was 62 years old when she retired from her management job at a circuit board manufacturing company in Williamsport, Pennsylvania. Her first move was to get rid of her "old woman's car" and buy a sports car. She cut her hair, started wearing makeup and promptly embarked on an adventure she'd been dreaming of for years: non-stop travel. She was on the road for a year, touring Israel, Canada, the Caribbean, Alaska and most of the southern United States.

But despite the fact that she'd anticipated spending most of her retirement in a state of non-stop travel, she discovered at the end of the year that life as a tourist wasn't all it was cracked up to be. So she returned home and tried to adjust to life as a retiree—sleeping in, volunteering and enjoying the comforts of her home. Then Christmas happened.

It wasn't much different from the dozens of Christmases that had gone before it. "All the children came to my house for Christmas Day, because that was our tradition," she says. Her husband had died some years earlier, but her five children, sixteen grandchildren and many great-grandchildren, along with assorted friends and family members, still came to her house for Christmas dinner. She had spent days buying and wrapping Christmas presents, planning a menu, buying food and preparing the meal. She fed seventy-five people that day. And when the last of her brood left, Arlene collapsed into bed.

"I was totally, completely exhausted," she remembers. "And I remember crying and asking God, 'Is this really what it's all about?'" Like many families, Arlene's was experiencing the difficulty of maintaining its traditional family Christmas gathering. Everyone was busy with their lives and may have preferred to spend the holiday in the quiet of their own homes. Arlene may have preferred to spend the day reading or praying, rather than on her feet, cooking. "But no one could say no because it was tradition."

So on that pivotal Christmas evening, Arlene prayed for something new. As the eldest of seven children, and a mother to five, she'd spent decades caring for other people. Now she was ready to embrace her newfound freedom. She prayed and prayed—and ultimately learned that the answers to our prayers aren't always what we imagine them to be.

Through the Methodist Church, Arlene learned about a non-profit-run refugee camp in the Democratic Republic of Congo, and she decided to volunteer. She had never been to the African continent before but felt called to go. "Ignorance was bliss," she says.

She travelled first to Goma, a dangerous part of the country. While she felt protected within the confines of the camp, when she travelled with her colleagues from one region to another, their vehicle would be shot at. After three months of volunteering, the eruption of a nearby volcano forced Arlene and her colleagues over the border into Rwanda. And there she discovered a land she would not be able to leave.

Arlene encountered children who were coming back to their home country after having been refugees in the Congo following the Rwandan genocide. While some would be reunited with their parents, many were not. Arlene realized that in many cases, "there was nowhere for the children to go, and no facilities where they'd be taken care of."

In the next few years, over the course of numerous trips between Africa and the United States, Arlene began collecting items for the children and raising money for aid. In 2004, she created the Urukundo Foundation and built the Urukundo Home for Children. Originally Arlene's plan was that the home would be for vulnerable girls ages 7 and over. "I was a great-grandmother and I had determined that I wasn't going to have any babies here."

Then one evening the vice-mayor of the town and a policeman knocked on the door of the home Arlene had purchased. The policeman was holding a four-month-old infant boy. "This baby needs a home—can you help?" the mayor asked her.

"I could not turn that baby away," says Arlene.

Today that little boy, David, is in the first grade. He lives in the Urukundo Home for Children with twenty-three other children under the age of 7. There are twenty-seven older children who attend nearby boarding schools (common for secondary-school-aged students in Rwanda). Arlene provides a safe home for children who have been abandoned, orphaned, abused or living in bad circumstances. What began as an acre compound grew to a twelve-acre compound. The Urukundo Foundation and its U.S.-based fundraising arm, a non-profit named Hope Made Real, have established an elementary school that educates not only the children in the Urukundo Home, but also kids from the surrounding community. Of the 195 children in the school, only fifteen are from the home. The school boasts the very first school library in the area. There is a dental services initiative that has provided free dental care to more than six thousand people. There is a sewing centre that teaches young girls how to sew so that they can get jobs. There is a chicken farm, as well as goats, pigs and rabbits. They sell eggs and milk in the community. They have also created a well and clean-water facility for the community. In total the Urukundo Foundation employs forty-five Rwandans and is the biggest employer in the area.

"We are making a difference, for the older people, the young people, and the entire community. It's the most incredible thing that anybody could be part of. And you can be part of it—you don't have to be rich or special. I'm neither. You just have to have a heart and a purpose and do it."

Speaking with Arlene over Skype is like watching a game of musical chairs as little Rwandan children wander into her office to sit on her lap, or cuddle in close as they ask her questions in perfect, Pennsylvania-accented English. Retirement, for Arlene, has offered up the unexpected. In her previous role as a manager, she had sworn that once she retired she'd sleep in every day. Instead, she wakes up most mornings at four a.m. to do computer work while the children sleep. Her life isn't what she had thought it would be—and she adores it.

"My life in Africa has been a tremendous adventure—like a second life," Arlene says. Running a non-profit, a school and a home for children has drawn upon the skills she built up as a mother, a nurse and a manager. "I'm no hero—I still have a short temper and little patience. But I wake up every day and thank God for my life. I've never felt happier or more alive."

Retiring from her job didn't mean she had to "retire from life," Arlene says. And while she misses her children and wishes she could visit more (she lives on her social security pension and puts any additional money she has into her foundation), she believes she is right where she needs to be. "My family doesn't need a great-grandmother. They don't need someone they pull out on special occasions, pat on the head, and then say, 'I'll pull you out on the next family occasion.' This is not the life for any grown woman or man. Freedom starts after age 65. That's when our real life's work begins."

Arlene's story is powerful and instructive in so many ways.

Her example provides a lesson in how pursuing adventure in our third act can be a gift to ourselves and also to the world. Arlene— who is now well into her eighties—swears the fruits of her African adventure make her feel younger each year. "It's an unending journey because my life changes each day."

Through adventure, Betty Steinhauer, Arlene Brown and women like them have found a vehicle to give back to society. And experts like Dr. Martha Beck suggest that breaking the mould of our lives through new adventures is also a way to cope with the startling pace at which our society is changing. As a Harvard-trained sociologist, Dr. Beck examines broad social trends, and what she sees in today's world is unique. "We are living in a radically shifting socioeconomic landscape. We've reached a point of social change that is completely unprecedented in the history of humanity," she says.

Because of this immense change, Dr. Beck says many of her clients come to her anxious and afraid about how to cope. "The problem is that sometimes older people keep going back to the patterns or structures that worked when they were younger." For instance, the woman who has been laid off from her old job tries to find a new job doing exactly the same tasks in a very similar organization, rather than looking for ways to apply her skills in new and interesting ways. "To survive amidst this scale of change, we need to adapt and create new opportunities for ourselves," says Dr. Beck, and the way to do that is to seek fresh experiences.

Annette Verschuren did just that when she turned down

lucrative offers from major retail corporations who wanted her to replicate her tremendous success in building Home Depot. Instead, she forged her own path, venturing into the world of entrepreneurship. The move jolted her out of a year-long retirement into a new career that not only excites her, but has helped make her "happier than she has ever been."

Maybe you've never considered yourself the bold and adventurous type. Perhaps you've always been a creature of routine. I have learned to love routine. And yet, as we get older, adventure, novelty and growth become utterly necessary for our survival, vibrancy and brain health, says psychiatrist Dr. Tony Phillips. "The brain loves stimulus and novelty," he says. "It seeks challenge." Finding simple ways to introduce adventure into your life—driving home by a different route, exploring neighbourhoods you've never seen, taking classes—can all provide your brain and soul with the stimulus it needs to carry you through older adulthood.

Role models can also help. Hearing stories from women like Annette, Betty and Arlene remind me of the transformative power of adventure. And the more we share such stories, the more we offer women social permission to seek adventure themselves.

"It's incredibly important that as women we own our desires," says Resa Eisen. Traditional roles and expectations of women have bestowed upon us a legacy of putting the needs and desires of other people first. And while this may serve a practical purpose at other life stages, when time is in drastically short supply, suppressing our desires can kill our quest for adventure and renewal later in life, says Eisen. So if you do crave adventure, the first step is to give yourself permission to pursue your dreams and whims. Says Dr. Beck: "Pay attention to your impulses, and give yourself permission to follow that inner compass."

Bucket Lists and Unfinished Business

In some cases, what the compass is urging you to do might seem impossible. At least it did in marathon swimmer Diana Nyad's case. But she found a way.

In the 1970s, Diana was one of the world's top marathon swimmers. In 1975, when she was 26 years old, she gained national recognition by swimming forty-five kilometres around Manhattan in just under eight hours. A few years later she set a world record in a 164-kilometre swim from the Bahamas to Florida. And then in 1978, she made her first attempt at what would be a lifelong pursuit: the swim from Cuba to Florida, described by many marathon swimmers as one of the most gruelling courses in the world. Since the 1950s, some of the world's best swimmers had attempted the swim without the aid of a shark cage. None had made it.

She left the Cuban shores on August 13. Roughly forty-two hours and 122 kilometres later, strong winds forced her to abandon the attempt. She did not, however, abandon her dream.

In 2010, at the age of 61, Diana began training again for the Cuba–Florida swim. A rash of experts including neurologists, sports therapists and even some members of her support team told her it was impossible. She disagreed. She completed eight-, ten-, twelve- and fourteen-hour swims every other week. Then she moved on to twenty-four-hour, open-water swims. On August 7, 2011, she began her second attempt to make the crossing. Strong winds and currents pushed her kilometres off course, and her asthma flared up, leaving her capable of doing only a few strokes at a time before she was forced to roll onto her back to catch her breath. Eventually, she was forced to concede. Over the next two years, Diana would make two more attempts to cross the open ocean. Each time she failed, due to strong winds, storms and jellyfish stings.

On August 31, 2013, Diana decided to give her lifelong dream one last try. She made the trip with an entourage of thirty people, including physicians, trainers and experts on sharks and jellyfish. She swam without a shark cage but wore a full-body silicon suit, gloves, face mask and booties to protect her from potentially deadly box jellyfish. Her team carried water and food, but to ensure her swim was "unassisted," she was not permitted to touch the boat or directly touch her team members at any time while she was in the water.

As she would later recount, Diana's fifty-three-hour swim was an "epic journey," filled with highs and lows. Her face, lips, even her throat swelled from salt water, which made breathing difficult. At night she swam without lights, as these attracted sharks and jellyfish. Her entourage travelled on a blacked-out flotilla, keeping tabs on her by listening to the slap of her arms against the water.

Though she was in top physical condition, marathon swimming experts suggest that mental toughness is the most important factor in determining success in such extreme events. And Diana had plenty of that. To combat psychological isolation and physical pain and exhaustion, she kept a mental playlist of more than eighty songs. She sang John Lennon's "Imagine" a thousand times over in her head. She hallucinated, imagining she saw the Taj Mahal in the water. And when the journey became so difficult she wanted to give up, she repeated a mantra in her mind: *Find a way.*

She and her team had an agreement—they would never tell Diana how far she'd travelled or how close she was to land. But nearly two days into the swim, when her best friend and "handler," Bonnie Stoll (herself a former nationally ranked raquetball player), saw Diana struggling, she called out to her, urging her to look ahead. Diana lifted her head out of the water, and in the distance she saw a line of white light. She thought it was first light. Bonnie told her it was the lights of Key West.

For the next fifteen hours, Diana says, she turned off her inner playlist and began reflecting instead on why she had attempted this epic adventure after four failed attempts, and at age 64, a point at which even her most ardent supporters believed the goal was likely out of reach. "It wasn't the ego . . . it was deeper . . . let's face it, we're all on a one-way street," she said during a 2014 TED talk. "What are we going to do to ensure we have no regrets looking back?"

Swimming on the open ocean, surrounded by azure blue in all directions, Diana said she was overcome by the beauty. "To feel the majesty of this blue planet we live on" was life-affirming and unforgettable, she said. And while she'd attempted the swim in her twenties, her final attempt had a distinct motivation. "It wasn't about that concrete, 'Can you do it?'" she said. Instead, it was about reaching for the horizon. Attempting something, even though she knew she might fail. "What a tremendous build of character and spirit . . . what a foundation you lay down in reaching for those horizons."

Exhausted and dehydrated, Diana staggered to shore in Key West fifty-three hours after she had started the swim. At 64 years old, she became the first person ever to successfully complete the journey. Today, Diana says, "[There is] no doubt in my mind that I am at the prime of my life . . . You can chase your dreams at any age . . . Never, ever give up."

Diana's incredible TED talk, combined with your own inner craving for growth and adventure, might just inspire you to do something fun, novel, or even drastic. As her story underscores, adventure can be a powerful vehicle for self-actualization and fulfillment regardless of our age.

How to "Do" Adventure

Therapist Resa Eisen says that the women who meet the greatest challenges indulging their desire for adventure are "the ones who are looking for something so completely out of their experience." On the other hand, the women for whom adventure or growth is more of an aligned evolution from their current life have an easier time because "they've already been successful [in a related area], so they know how to maximize that and take it to the next level." This doesn't mean that we all need to pursue adventures that line up with our current lives. Rather, it means we need to break our vast desires into smaller chunks as we take steps toward our goals.

Let's look at the woman who wanted to climb Everest and move to a remote country for six months. She ran into serious resistance from her children, who thought the idea crazy, and from her husband, who didn't want to move and felt six months apart was too long. So together, Eisen and the woman came up with an alternative plan that still fulfilled her need for change and adventure: travelling to a remote country for several weeks rather than several months.

"It's not that the original goal wasn't a great one," says Eisen. The point was to start by scaling back the goal so that it could be achieved, while still taking steps in the direction the woman wanted to go. When women want to pursue big, seemingly impossible dreams, Eisen encourages them to step back, "look at the opportunities and possibilities and explore how to do it creatively, rather than shelve a big dream and ultimately be unhappy and resentful."

The world of business also offers examples of how we might pursue—and achieve—large-scale dreams. And while you and I might not be dreaming of launching multi-million dollar enterprises, we can certainly borrow tactics from those whose goal is entrepreneurial growth.

In his book *Double Double*, author and consultant Cameron Herold, the Canadian former chief operating officer of 1-800-Got-Junk, lays out a blueprint for how to achieve significant gains. One of the first steps, he advises growth-seekers, is to "lean out" into the future and imagine exactly what their daily lives will be like once they have achieved their goal. This visualization technique is frequently used by athletes and other performers. I enjoy watching the Olympics, and before a race, I'll often see the runners deep in thought, staring down the track, making little movements as though they are actually running the race. Clearly, visualization helps elite athletes achieve their goals—why not you and me?

Next, Herold suggests that you take a few pieces of loose-leaf paper, find a quiet, out-of-the-way place such as a local library or café, and spend an hour or so creating what he calls a Painted Picture—a vividly described, detail-rich account of a day in your life a few months or years down the road, in which your dream has been fulfilled. It's critically important when creating your Painted Picture not to get too caught up in the "how," but to get crystal clear on what you actually want. Eisen might call this step "owning our desires."

After you've created your Painted Picture—which is usually a three- to four-page document—Herold advises you to read it frequently, as a reminder of the life you are aiming to create. The next step is to "reverse-engineer" your dreams. The term *reverse-engineer* means to study something closely and figure out exactly how it was built so that you may build it yourself. In the case of your Painted Picture, you work backwards, figuring out precisely what projects, initiatives or steps you need to undertake in order to reach your goal.

When you've identified the appropriate projects, it's time to set a series of small goals for each. In the case of the woman who wanted to live in a remote country for six months, a small goal was to identify a not-so-remote country and live there for several weeks.

Herold advises that goals should be SMART:

S stands for shared. Sharing our goals with others enables us to get the support we need to reach them.
M stands for measurable. For instance, "I want to lose weight" is vague. "I want to lose five pounds" is measurable.

A stands for attainable. The goal needs to be at least "remotely possible," as Herold writes.

R stands for relevant. Ask: Is this goal truly meaningful to you? Is it worth taking on? You might want to lose some weight, for example, but there may be other goals far more important to you.

T stands for time-bound. Deadlines give structure to plans.

Imagine your dream is to run a marathon. You might create a vivid Painted Picture that details how you rise at daybreak, drink a nutrient-rich smoothie and then go for a vigorous run through quiet streets, taking in the beauty of the dawning day. You then eat a nutritious breakfast, go for a well-deserved massage and so on.

Next, you reverse-engineer your Painted Picture. If you've never run a race before, your first goal might be to find a running coach to help you design a training program; your second, to work with a nutritionist; your third, to create a three-month training program; and your fourth, to run your first ten-kilometre race by a specific date.

By dreaming in detail, identifying important projects or actions, and then setting a series of SMART goals, your big dreams and adventures can be reverse-engineered into small, doable steps.

Coming down the Mountain

One of the recurring themes in the stories of women adventurers I've recounted here—indeed, an important theme throughout this book—is that support is critical. To pursue our dreams, seek adventure and live our best lives, we absolutely need help. This lesson has been brought home to me time and again throughout my life.

A few months after I gave birth to Ally, we took a family ski trip to Whistler—my favourite ski destination in the entire world. Justin and I were skiing "the Saddle"—a bold and particularly beautiful run. One of the most thrilling parts of the run is a three-metre cliff drop, at the bottom of which on the day in question lay a thick blanket of fluffy snow. I'd made the jump dozens of times before, but on this day, I halted. I simply couldn't do it. As a new mother, I was feeling my mortality keenly, and something inside me simply would not let me make the jump. I stood frozen in place on the hill, unable to move. I had come to the mountain seeking adventure, but suddenly I had no idea how I would get down.

Justin, who was skiing behind me, stopped. "I can't do the jump," I told him. "I honestly can't do it." He talked to me, encouraging me to follow him as he took another trail that would get us down the hill. Alone in my fear, I hadn't been able to see any alternatives.

I don't wish to climb Mount Everest, nor do I want to start a thriving business. But I do want adventure to be as much a part of my third act as it was the earlier part of my life. I feel a strong pull toward my work bringing fresh drinking water and sanitation to the poorest regions of Africa, and pursuing this passion is, I believe, where my future adventures lie.

Empowerment

Adventure has long been, for me, intricately connected to empowerment. When Pierre and I were living at 24 Sussex, Gloria Steinem sent me a present. It was a subscription to *Ms.*, the liberal feminist magazine Steinem had co-founded. I was delighted; I had always considered myself a feminist, and the magazine encouraged me at a time when I felt imprisoned by my role as a first lady. Pierre, however, was less impressed. He did not think *Ms.* belonged at 24 Sussex.

It seems ironic that the man who established Canada's Charter of Rights and Freedoms would take issue with his wife reading *Ms.* For all his ideals, I think that Pierre, like many men of his generation, believed that true equality stopped at the front door. A woman might be a feminist outside the home, but *inside* the home? That sort of power was far too disruptive.

I have seen tremendous social change during my lifetime. In some ways, it feels like only yesterday that I graduated from university. And yet, back then it was assumed that once a well-educated, career-oriented woman married, she would soon quit her job to stay home and raise children. There were many women who bucked this trend, but a majority of us fulfilled the social expectations and obligations of the time: that a woman's place was in the home. This is no longer a commonly held expectation. Today women constitute the majority in many advanced degree programs. In increasing numbers, young women are exercising the freedom that previous generations helped win—the freedom of choice. There are many works that examine the progress and challenges of feminism in our long march toward equality. I do not wish to replicate this body of work. Suffice it to say: when it comes to feminism, though much has been achieved, the road is still long.

What I wish to explore further, however, is our collective ability to take what we and other generations have fought so hard to win and truly *use* that freedom to live the lives of our choice. What I want to explore is the personal, intimate side of feminism, and the way in which this sweeping social change that has been such an integral part of my generation's legacy is experienced at the level of the heart. What I'm talking about, of course, is empowerment.

Leaning In, with Love

One of the most influential recent books about women's empowerment is *Lean In*, written by Facebook's chief operating officer, Sheryl Sandberg. In her book, Sandberg offers a plethora of useful career advice for women. But one of the ideas that intrigued me most was her insight about the implications of home life. Sandberg wrote, "I truly believe that the single most important career decision that a woman makes is whether she will have a life partner and who that partner is. I don't know of a single woman in a leadership position whose life partner is not fully— and I mean fully—supportive of her career. No exceptions."

What Sandberg articulates here is, I believe, the same issue that underlay Pierre's displeasure with *Ms.* The battle for true empowerment may end up at corporate boards and the upper echelons of power. But it begins at home.

Our closest intimate relationships are among the most

fundamental influencers in our lives. When we do not feel we can truly be ourselves in these relationships, we cannot hope to live empowered lives. As much as I loved and respected my two husbands, and as much as I love the institution of marriage, I found marriage to be a type of prison. We had some happy times together, but in both cases I inevitably came to feel trapped by the bonds of these close relationships. Was my mental illness a factor? Without a doubt. But the fact remains that while I may experience loneliness as a single woman, I also experience a great degree of personal freedom; I am the captain of my own ship. I know that if I am unhappy, I have no one to blame but myself.

There are other, highly successful women who have found relationships that support their empowerment. Annette Verschuren now works full-time at the energy storage company she founded but also commits a significant amount of time to charities and corporate boards, and routinely spends time on the weekends attending to work. "These are fun things to do," she says. "I'm like a kid in a candy store. My husband understands that. He gets me."

For Annette, the ability to find a partner who supports her empowered lifestyle came after the breakdown of her first marriage and a decade spent on her own. The years she spent as a single woman helped her to understand her wants and needs, and to take complete responsibility for creating a life she wanted. "I make my life—I don't wait for people to come to me," she remarks.

Many of the women interviewed for this book offer similar insight. Older adulthood is a stage of life where, if you're lucky, you have unprecedented freedom. But in order to truly exercise the benefits of freedom, we must take responsibility for articulating our desires and taking action to achieve them. True empowerment, remarks Annette, "is an attitude"—a belief that the woman calling the shots is you.

The Price of Freedom

Freedom gives us the responsibility of choice. And the downside of having choice is potentially living with guilt or regret. A 2014 interview of PepsiCo's Indra K. Nooyi by David Bradley, the owner of *The Atlantic*, throws the price of choice into sharp relief.

Indra relates a story about the day the board of directors of the soft-drink company named her CEO. Rather than staying at work until midnight, which was her normal routine, she came home at ten p.m. to share the news with her husband and her mother, who lived with them.

"Mom, I've got great news for you," Indra said as she walked in the door.

"Let the news wait," her mother said. "Can you go out and get some milk?" Indra's mother hadn't wanted to ask her son-in-law—who had arrived home much earlier—to get milk because he was "tired." When Indra came home from the milk run grumbling that she'd been trying to celebrate the biggest day of her career, her mother shot back with this: "You might be president of PepsiCo. You might be on the board of directors. But when you enter this house, you're the wife, you're the daughter, you're the daughter-in-law, you're the mother. You're all of that. Nobody else can take that place. So leave that damned crown in the garbage. And don't bring it into the house."

Indra went on to explain the sense of guilt she has experienced over the years as her high-powered job—a role she loves—has at times taken her away from her family and children. "You have to cope," she said. "Because you die with guilt. You just die with guilt."

I adore Indra's honesty in outlining the price she has paid in pursuit of her dreams. She is a trailblazer and a much-needed role model for ambitious women of all ages. But I would respectfully point out that no matter how outwardly successful a person may be, "dying with guilt" does not an empowered woman make.

Yet Indra offers an example of a challenge so many women face: How best to move forward when many choices are available to us? And how to move forward with a light and optimistic heart, with the knowledge of the paths not taken? I certainly have experienced my fair share of guilt. For instance, when I first left Pierre, I needed time to establish myself not only in a career but also in an independent life. This would require time and distance, and Pierre and I decided he would take over main custody of the boys for a brief period while I restarted my life outside 24 Sussex. On the one hand, I felt proud of myself for having taken this much-needed step and for establishing my independence. On the other hand, I experienced terrible guilt at having left my young boys for a time—even if it was in the care of their loving father.

I made my decision in response to a deep need I felt at the time—a need for independence. But I certainly struggled with guilt over my decision. In this way, I am perhaps not so different from Indra, who chose to pursue her dreams as a business leader but experienced guilt over that decision. Empowerment, then, has a lot to do with understanding *how* to make good decisions—and live guilt-free with the consequences. The world of business—which routinely calculates the returns on various leadership decisions—offers some applicable insight. In a 2010 article for the *Harvard Business Review,* Jonathan Doochin, the chair of the Leadership Institute at Harvard College, describes the link between good decision-making and a company's ability to keep its overarching values at the forefront: managers can create more effective teams "by turning to their personal and organizational values."

Of course, in order to put your values at the forefront, you first need to understand what those values are. As a younger woman, I had little "mental white space" to carefully consider my values. They lived within me, of course, but in many ways, I held my values unconsciously. To an extent, I still do. Taking the time to write down your top five values—be they independence, honesty, achievement, freedom or whatever else you hold dear—and then considering how a potential decision stacks up against these values is a useful exercise.

Put Your Values to Work

A truly empowered woman transforms her values into verbs. She understands what she values most, and she takes steps to bring that value to life. This is a lifelong challenge. And as older adults, endowed with life experience, wisdom, skills and time, we are in a unique position to put our values to work. Perhaps it's because I grew up with so many sisters, but I have long held a belief that the world will be changed by women helping other women.

Have we truly fulfilled the transformation we set out to achieve in the 1960s? Perhaps. Though great social changes have occurred in the last five decades, more work is needed. As women, we are being called upon to reshape the world. This aim begins at the level of the individual woman who, in her heart of hearts, gives herself permission to own her desires, act upon her ambitions and use her skills in the service of others. I cannot think of a worthier goal than that.

CHAPTER 4

THE BONDS THAT SUSTAIN US

Nurture your connections to the people who matter most.

If there is one lesson I have learned over the course of my life, it is this: we cannot do it alone. Relationships are life-giving and life-supporting. Of all I have accumulated these last sixty-odd years, my relationships are what I hold most precious. My relationships with my children and grandchildren, with my two husbands, with my sisters and with my friends have all nourished and protected me from the ravages and challenges of my life. At the same time, they have deepened my most joyful and celebratory moments. Friendships have helped to soothe and calm my inner life during dark and turbulent hours. My relationships with my children have taught me profound lessons about adulthood and the human condition. In short, my relationships have shaped who I am and who I am still becoming.

When it comes to living a vibrant life as an older adult,

studies show that friendships are indispensible. In 1976, Harvard University researchers began the landmark Nurses' Health Study, established by Drs. Frank Speizer and Walter Willett. The purpose was to investigate an array of factors that affect women's health, with particular focus on cancer prevention. More than 238,000 nurses participated. The researchers discovered that the more friends a woman has, the less likely she is to develop physical impairments as she ages, and the more likely she is to experience joy. The most stunning finding: researchers suggested that the role of close friendships is so significant that *not* having close confidantes is as detrimental to a woman's health as smoking or being overweight.

The costs of social isolation are high—across virtually all of the chronic illnesses affecting older adults, from cancer and arthritis to depression and neurodegenerative disease, maintaining social networks and nurturing relationships is regarded as a key preventive measure. "Having someone you can confide in helps prevent depression and helps you recover from depression," says Dr. Marie-France Rivard, a geriatric psychiatrist and professor of psychiatry at the University of Ottawa. Another study found that people with no friends increased their risk of death over a six-month period, while another study found that people with the most friends over a nine-year period reduced their chance of premature death by almost two-thirds.

In a 2002 breakthrough study on friendship among women, UCLA researchers discovered that women's propensity to form a network of close relationships may be one of the reasons we live longer than men. And fittingly, the genesis of the study was a joking conversation between Drs. Shelley Taylor and Laura Klein about how differently women researchers behaved when stressed compared to their male counterparts. It was a long-standing joke that when women researchers were stressed, they came into the lab, cleaned it up and bonded with other researchers over coffee. When the men were stressed, they tended to hole up in some private area of the lab. One day, Dr. Taylor and Dr. Klein got talking about how as much as 90 percent of the research on stress was conducted on men.

Over the course of their work together, Dr. Taylor and Dr. Klein made a stunning discovery: women respond to stress very differently than men do. Before the study, scientists thought that stress triggered within *all* humans a freeze or flee response. And while this is typically true in men, the UCLA study found that in women, stress triggers the release of oxytocin. Also known as the "love hormone," oxytocin is released after childbirth and serves multiple purposes—it shrinks the uterus, stimulates milk production, promotes mother–baby bonding and also induces that feeling of euphoria that (almost) makes you forget about the pain you've just endured.

According to Dr. Taylor and Dr. Klein's research, when oxytocin is released as part of the stress response in women, it triggers a "tend and befriend" response, encouraging a woman either to tend to her children or loved ones, or to gather other women around her. The positive feelings induced by tending and befriending release yet more oxytocin, which creates further feelings of calm, connection and safety. In men, however, stress tends to trigger the release of testosterone, which impedes the calming properties of oxytocin.

One of the biggest stressors older women can face is the death of a spouse. When the UCLA researchers examined the role of friendships among women who had recently been widowed, they discovered that those with close friendships were more likely to get through the experience without negative health outcomes.

I know the "tend and befriend" response well. In fact, the term conjures in my mind the memory of my dear friend Lady Mary Mitchell and her lovely villa in Jamaica.

Pierre and I were all set to travel to Jamaica for a state trip in 1972 when the high commissioner informed us that the hotel where we were staying didn't permit babies. (Today it probably even allows pets.) We were put instead in a guest house on the estate of Sir Harold and Lady Mary Mitchell. And thus began one of the most nurturing and enriching friendships of my life. Sir Harold was a former United Kingdom Conservative MP. Lady Mary was originally Mary Pringle, an heiress to the Pringle of Scotland company, internationally renowned for its beautiful cashmere sweaters. I didn't see much of Sir Harold during that visit, but Lady Mary was an absolute delight. She was worldly, interesting and smart. She counted the playwright Noel Coward among her close friends. From the moment I met her, I fell in love with her in the way we can only love a friend—I sat at her feet, listened to her stories and felt reassured. She saw the strain I was experiencing in my marriage, and she lent a listening ear, showing incredible sympathy, offering sage advice, but never taking sides. I trusted her completely.

Lady Mary ran her estate with little fuss; the meals were simple and excellent, all prepared, she said, by "Mrs. MacFarlane." When midafternoon came, she'd head back to the big house from where we'd been chatting at our villa, claiming she'd ask Mrs. MacFarlane to make us G&Ts "without the tonic." I remember one evening during that trip, a bishop came to visit. Lady Mary loved to dance—as did I—and we had resolved to head down to a nearby dance club that evening. "But first," she said, "we must put the bishop to bed." She always had her priorities in order.

I went back year after year, as did Pierre, even after our breakup. Lady Mary's estate became an oasis of calm for me. It was not simply on account of the luxurious surroundings and fantastic weather. It was because of Lady Mary, and our wonderful relationship. To this day I miss our friendship deeply.

Women like Lady Mary have been an incredible source of strength for me. While my younger adulthood was filled with challenges, I always had plenty of time to nurture my friendships—and for that I'm grateful. But that is not always the case, point out Drs. Terri Apter and Ruthellen Josselson in their book *Best Friends: The Pleasure and Perils of Girls' and Women's Friendships.* In fact, they point out that when women become stressed or busy, one of the first things we eliminate from our schedules is our time with friends.

Make Time for Friends

I have made many mistakes in my life, and failing to keep up with friends has been one of my biggest. The best version of me has a deeply held knowledge that in order to remain mentally healthy, I must maintain my social networks. In fact, the only time I have let relationships go is when I have been in the throes of either depression or mania. Unfortunately, until recently that was quite often. Since my recovery, I have tried hard to keep in touch with old friends and make new ones too.

One of the ways I keep up my friendships is the good old-fashioned telephone. Almost every day, I try to call a close friend for a conversation. My friends are scattered all over the world, and telephone conversations offer a wonderful way for us to stay connected and provide emotional support to each other even though thousands of kilometres may separate us.

Another way I have maintained strong friendships has been to allot visiting time when I travel. It's easy, while travelling, to be away for no more time than is necessary to visit your family members, attend a conference or otherwise fulfill the main purpose of your trip. There is often some inexplicable pull homeward. I have learned to ensure I always leave time to visit friends. So for instance, when I travel to Ottawa to visit Justin and Sophie, I always try to see at least a few of my dear Ottawa friends.

Women have different types of friends, says Margaret Critchlow, an anthropologist and trainer in healthy aging-in-place courses—courses that teach older adults how to live well in their homes so they don't need to move into a nursing home. There are old, old friends with whom you share a bond that may go back decades. And there are new friends who infuse your life with excitement and new energy. Finding and nurturing both is incredibly important. "We spend so much time working on financial plans but almost no time working on friendship plans," says Critchlow. In her workshops, Critchlow urges participants to regard their social connections in the same way they regard their investment portfolios. "You have blue-chip friends and growth stocks," she says. "You have to invest in both."

Blue-chip friendships are those that have been forged over time and through shared experience. You trust each other deeply and know each other intimately, and because of this, Critchlow says, you reap a "steady return on investment" from each other in terms of mutual encouragement, understanding and support. When I think of blue-chip friends, I think of Vicky Wilgress, and the girlfriends I first met years ago at the Parent Resource Centre in Ottawa.

Ottawa is a beautiful city, but I have a complicated relationship with the place. It's where my children were born, and it has also borne witness to the most challenging periods of my life. During my time as the prime minister's wife and for a period afterward, I found it difficult to make friends. I was vulnerable, and I worried that I would not be able to trust the people I met, or that I was being unfairly judged. I was lonely.

Following Kyle's birth, I began taking him to the resource centre to participate in playgroups and other programs. Over a few months of showing up consistently, I formed friendships with some of the other mothers. While our children played together, we talked about books, our marriages, money, food, great restaurants, music and so on. Someone decided we should move playgroup from the centre into our homes. Then, once the children were in school, we met for book club one evening a month. These women were a tremendous source of support to me during my illness and after the deaths of Michel and Pierre. They filled my freezer with food and soup, they sat with me while I cried, and they continued to show up even after I insisted that I was fine.

These shared experiences have created a strong bond between us. They truly are my blue-chip friends—I'll nurture and protect those friendships forever.

Growth-stock friendships are a little different, but no less important to your health. They are newer friendships with people you are powerfully drawn to. "You invest a little bit of energy into the relationship and it tends to grow quickly," says Critchlow. The beauty of these friendships is that they offer inspiration, new ideas and opportunities to expand. Take my friend Nancy. We have been friends for only a few years, and we take pleasure in each other's diverse perspectives. While I was home raising children, Nancy was forging a high-powered career. We each bring a unique viewpoint to the friendship, and getting to know one another has been fun.

Nancy's newest venture is a sprawling farm north of Toronto. I went to visit her recently, imagining we would have a relaxing weekend, sipping lemonade on her patio as we took in the sweep of fields surrounding the house. This is likely the experience I might have had on a weekend visit with one of my blue-chip friends. Not so in Nancy's case. After a lovely—if bumpy—tour of her property in her Gator, we spent the rest of the time at work: cooking up hundreds of pounds of rhubarb into rhubarb jam, stringing up tomato vines and hand-watering acres of vegetables for her vegetable stall in a nearby farmers' market. The work was gruelling, and not something I normally do. My arms were sore for days. And yet, the novelty of the experience was challenging, invigorating and wonderful. It was the stuff of growth-stock friends.

Diversity among friends is important. It's easy to find yourself surrounded with people who are exactly like you—perhaps the same age, socioeconomic level or sharing the same interests. But by expanding your network to include friends with different backgrounds, you expand and support mental well-being, says Dr. Anna Kudak, author of *What Happy Women Do,* in a 2012 interview with MSN. "Friendships with older and younger people help broaden your perspective, which in turn allows you to have compassion and empathy in your day-to-day life."

According to Dr. Suzanne Degges-White, co-author of *Friends Forever: How Girls and Women Forge Lasting Relationships,* while many solid friendships begin the way mine did at the Parent Resource Centre in Ottawa—between people who share similar interests or life circumstances—the ones that deepen and grow are always built on mutual trust, compassion, honesty and unconditional acceptance. I welcome opportunities to spend time with younger people. For instance, my sons often invite me up for big celebrations at their family property at Morin-Heights. They also invite their own friends. Spending time with younger people is a fabulous antidote to the perils of aging, I've found. But nurturing friendships with older people can be every bit as rewarding. For instance, Drs. Lawrence Weiss and Marjorie Lowenthal, from the University of California, concluded that older adults perceive the complexity in situations more than younger people do, which can make us valuable and astute friends. I think of my lovely friend Martine, who, in her late eighties, still cycles twenty kilometres on a weekend, and devotes herself to learning new languages to keep herself sharp. And there is something comforting about having friends who are significantly older than us; they offer a much-needed perspective that our contemporaries can rarely offer. Martine has travelled the world, had marriages, raised children, and she has also been alone. When I feel tired or scared or bored with myself, I call Martine, and she inspires me.

Make New Friends

So it's one thing to nurture existing friends. It's quite another to make new ones. Critchlow points out that the beauty of making friends as an older adult is that we are more confident, and often surer of ourselves and what we stand for. This can make it easier to form authentic relationships, although she suggests it can also make us more rigid. "It's important to remain open-minded," she points out. One way to do this is to take on new challenges, to remain outwardly focused by getting involved with new projects or activities. This is how Critchlow virtually doubled her circle of friends overnight.

She and a colleague had been discussing the idea of creating a co-housing facility in Sooke, B.C., for several years, until one day they decided it was time to take action. They booked a meeting room above a grocery store and posted notices around town. On the appointed evening, they arrived early, hoping at least one person would show up. In the end, more than thirty people came through the doors. Some were friends she and her colleague had known for years. Others were people she'd never met. Over the next few months, as the group crystallized and began creating a vision and plans for what their co-housing project would look like, they developed stronger friendships with one another. Through these relationships, Critchlow found she was beginning to pursue exciting new hobbies and activities she'd never imagined doing. For instance, one of the men who attended the co-housing meeting expressed a desire for the community to have a ropes course, an outdoor obstacle course made primarily of ropes and an activity for personal and team development. Critchlow was skeptical. So the man set up a ropes course for her and others to try. They had a blast.

By pursuing a new interest—the development of a co-housing unit—Critchlow says, "I'm doing more new things than I have done since I was a teenager." By remaining outwardly focused and committed to a growth curve, she has not only diversified her "social portfolio," but also fulfilled the promise of her generation. "We were going to change the world in the '60s," she says. "Now we are in our sixties and we finally have the time to do it." Finding friendships to nurture, energize and support us is critical to living a life rich in adventure and contribution, she says.

I couldn't agree more. My work as a brain health advocate has put me in contact with some of the country's leading practitioners in mental health and neuroscience. I am passionate about acquiring knowledge related to brain health, and so I have joined boards of national mental health organizations, and I speak at and attend mental health conferences as often as possible. These activities have helped me build my professional and personal networks. I enjoy running into colleagues at international conferences. I adore working the room at conference networking events, keeping my ears pricked for new research and groundbreaking studies. The professional friendships I have cultivated energize and renew me.

If you take an inventory of your friends and find you have plenty of blue-chip friends but too few growth stocks, consider taking up new activities, joining community groups or volunteering your time at organizations where you will have an opportunity to meet different people. New friendships can infuse our lives with vibrancy and excitement.

Recognize the Power of Friendship

In a culture that remains hyper-focused on youth, friendships can encourage us to contribute and create positive change. When Dr. Martha Beck moved from Arizona to California several years ago, she discovered a group of older women who, like her, loved horses and went out riding each week. She joined them. Their trail rides throughout the central coast region are characterized by a spirit of adventurousness and the quest for change, she says. The women talked about different groups they were organizing: book clubs, social activism organizations, Bible study sessions. "I realized that these older women were actually creating a backbone of social action."

There is power in women "ganging up." In 2001, two women from Wolfville, Nova Scotia, challenged each other to put on a production of *The Vagina Monologues*. They recruited some of their friends, who in turn recruited other friends, to perform and help with set creation, stage management, marketing and ticket sales. They performed to a sold-out crowd and donated the proceeds to charity. Since then, the Women of Wolfville have put on shows to sold-out crowds nearly every year, forming strong bonds of friendship while donating thousands of dollars to charity.

The playwright Eve Ensler, creator of *The Vagina Monologues*, is known for uniting women against sexual violence. In her stunning memoir, *In the Body of the World*, she relates how it was her friendships with other women that saw her through a devastating battle with uterine cancer.

As older adulthood brings with it the increased risks of poor health and loss, friendships provide us with the support we require to get through our challenges. Such is the power of friendship among women.

Adult Children: Choose a Way and Stick to It

As critical as our relationships with friends may be, the relationships we have with our children are important too. And these relationships go through profound changes as we age.

"Women sometimes struggle with the sense of always being a caretaker, being the protector, no matter where their kids are, what they're doing, or whether she has the capacity to be available to them," says family therapist Resa Eisen. And while this role makes sense when our children are small, it can become a liability as we get older, says Eisen. "The problems start when either the woman or the kids find it hard to separate."

How do you separate from a being to whom you have given life? I find this desperately difficult, and I know that other women struggle with it also. I have friends whose grown children complain they help too little, but there are many others out there, including grandmothers, who possibly help too much.

The best advice I ever received on the topic of helping grown children came from my mother's best friend from childhood. Aunty Joan is my godmother, and a wonderful lady. At 95 years of age, this tiny woman is as strong and determined as anything. She married early in life, as one did back then, and had four children. Her husband, a doctor, died very young, leaving her to raise her children alone.

There was always a no-frills, no-fantasy, stiff-upper-lip English quality to her that I loved. And yet, she was a firecracker: so engaging, alive and curious, always remembering everything about everyone and asking exactly the right questions. I used to take my mother there regularly, and Aunty Joan would serve up these perfect little baby sandwiches filled with butter and raisins. They were simply delicious. The last time I visited her we had a rousing discussion about politics. As I was leaving, she asked me a favour. "Margaret, could you please ask Justin to stop sending me emails? I've already given him all the money I'm allowed to donate." I told her I would put in a word—but didn't mention that I too get Justin's "Dear Margaret" emails.

When Aunty Joan became old enough that she no longer wanted to live alone, she added an efficient and private granny suite to the side of her home, with a separate entrance from outside, where she lives independently. She offered the main house to her daughter and her family. She is a political activist and wants the government to give more tax relief to families choosing to care for their elderly at home. Aunty Joan remains an integral part of her children's and grandchildren's lives, even offering an ironing service once a week to one daughter, an obligation she fulfills with cheer and precision.

I love the idea of choosing a way to help and sticking with it. After she graduated from university, my daughter, Ally, scored a wonderful position as a social media/marketing director at a chic company. The only problem was that her employer was located on the other side of the city. It would have taken her more than an hour to get to work via public transit, and I did not feel comfortable with her walking to the metro in the dark. So I offered to drive her. At first it seemed a little thing—a small favour to do for my youngest child. But over the past two years it has become a hefty commitment—well over two hours in the car each day, often battling rush-hour traffic. Then, of course, there's the cost of fuel and car repairs. But I chose to offer this help to my daughter, and I am happy to keep doing it. It makes me feel connected. We have valued time together each day. Through it all, Ally has been extremely appreciative. Still, I have been urging her to consider buying a car so that she can drive herself.

One of the challenges of parenting adult children is to do our best by them without enabling their dependence—or our own. The desire to help our kids can in some circumstances jeopardize our financial security over the long term. As with my decision to drive my daughter to work, these issues most always arise from the best of intentions.

Christine owned one of the most exclusive women's fashion boutiques in Ottawa. She began working at the store in the 1970s, and ultimately bought out the original owner and moved the entire store to a bigger, posher location on Sussex Drive. A couple of years ago, around the time her twenty-year lease was coming up for renewal, her son approached her and asked if she might consider transferring her lease to him. He had a successful business selling upscale home decor and saw an opportunity to grow the business with a second location. But not just any location. Watching his mother succeed in that swanky retail space had taught him the importance of real estate. He also asked if Christine would consider managing the store for him.

At the time, Christine was proud of the business she had built up, but she was feeling slightly bored and in need of a new challenge she could sink her teeth into. So she agreed. "I thought it would be an easy transition to close my store and work for my son. I would still be working with beautiful things and interacting with people."

So over the next few weeks, Christine sold off her stock, gave notice to her customers, transferred her lease to her son and closed down the business she had painstakingly built. She was sad to see the boutique go, but eager to start a new project and use her considerable skills and expertise to help her son.

When she showed up at work on the first day, she knew something was wrong the moment she saw her son's face. "He told me he'd decided to bring in his girlfriend to help manage the store." At first he'd thought his mother and girlfriend could work together. But his girlfriend had confessed to him that she didn't want to work with Christine. "It was my first day on the job working for my son and I got fired."

The anger and betrayal Christine felt was tempered by the love she felt for her son. "I was trying to be graceful about it," she says. "It's your child and you don't want to hurt him. You want him to succeed." And yet, with limited savings and now no source of income, Christine had allowed her desire to support her son's career to wreak havoc on her own financial future. As a resourceful and highly skilled woman, Christine has landed on her feet. After two years of hard work and much soul-searching she opened a new boutique, even better than the last. Her experience shows me the resilience she found within to get beyond the obstacles life threw at her.

Setting boundaries can be difficult. In fact, a 2008 study by R.D. Moremen, published in the *Journal of Women and Aging*, showed that most older women choose to avoid conflict rather than confront others about situations that hurt or disappoint them. And so rather than deal with the issue, we bear it quietly, which in turn makes us feel resentful or bitter. This response is the opposite of what we should be doing: long-lasting friendships are based on open, honest and authentic communication.

When setting boundaries with friends or loved ones, it's important to understand the mistaken beliefs that underlie a failure to be assertive, writes psychologist Dr. Martha Davis in her classic text, *The Relaxation and Stress Reduction Workbook.* For instance, a commonly held belief is that we should look after the needs of other people before our own. In reality, it is perfectly acceptable to put our own needs first sometimes. Another is that it's wrong to be antisocial, when, in fact, it's reasonable to wish to be alone at times. And yet another is that when people are in trouble, we should always help them. The truth: it isn't our responsibility to take ownership of other people's problems. Applying right thinking to the beliefs that keep us from respecting ourselves is an important step in becoming our own best friends.

Learning how to confront others is equally important. Like many people, I do not enjoy confrontation, but I have learned to make myself do it when necessary. In a Great Courses lecture series on effective communications, York University's Dr. Dalton Kehoe, a social psychologist, explains why we feel so uncomfortable confronting others. It all comes down to the cognitive unconscious—a part of the brain that processes information rapidly and helps us make the split-second decisions that can save our lives. For instance, the cognitive unconscious is at work when you move to cross the street but stop yourself just as a car barrels through the crosswalk. The executive functioning part of the brain, he argues, is far too slow and calculating for such a rapid response. But the cognitive unconscious cannot tell the difference between a physical threat and a threat to the ego. This is why we humans tend to exhibit specific fight or flight responses when we are in a heated exchange: rapid breathing, elevated heart rate, even a queasy or nauseated sensation in the stomach. Dr. Kehoe calls this response an "amygdala hijack," so named for the section of the brain—the amygdala—that is the source of much of our cognitive unconscious programming and that often takes over our rational mind in heated moments.

The key to overcoming an amygdala hijack is to breathe deeply in an effort to give the rational mind some time to "catch up." At that point, it's useful to have a structure with which to initiate a confrontation. In her book *Fierce Conversations*, executive coach Susan Scott provides a framework. The goal is to examine your thinking *before* you engage in the conversation, to present your issue clearly and then to spend most of your time listening to the other person in order to better understand them.

Scott suggests that before confronting someone, you do the following: name the issue as concisely as possible, determine the current impact on you and others, determine the future implications for you and others, examine your own contribution to the issue and describe the ideal outcome.

You can do this, or you can follow the "three strikes you're out" rule a friend of mine uses to protect her boundaries. When someone behaves in a hurtful or disrespectful manner, my friend will notify the person but mentally keep note of the "trespass." If a person makes two more "strikes," this friend simply moves away from the friendship. I admire her discipline, but I fear I'm too soft for that. I have made my share of mistakes—probably at least three for each friend. My focus is on enriching my relationships as much as I possibly can.

Boundaries are useful when it comes to engaging with our families. One of the enduring annoyances for many grandparents is the sense that we exist strictly as providers of free babysitting. I vividly recall the fatigue of parenthood—and the relative freedom my parents had just when I was living through one of life's busiest phases. But sometimes grandmothers simply don't *feel* like babysitting. I again borrow Aunty Joan's guideline, and try to be as useful as I can *within limits*. I live a few minutes away from Sacha, Zoë and their three gorgeous children, Pierre, Gala and Ariane. When it comes to babysitting, I specify that I will do it at my house, where I am surrounded by my own things and can totally relax once the little ones have gone to bed. I keep a drawer stocked with pyjamas, diapers and clothing so that we are never without the supplies we need. With boundaries in place, I feel free to give of my time and energy, knowing that I have been clear about what I will and won't do.

The most gorgeous part of babysitting grandchildren is that it provides an opportunity to rediscover your own inner child. Recently I was in Ottawa visiting Justin and Sophie and their children, Xavier, Ella-Grace and Hadrien. Xavier and Ella-Grace requested that I take them to a nearby play park. I agreed, thinking I would sit on a bench and watch them as they played. Ella-Grace had different ideas. She lured me onto the play structures, where I spent a few hours climbing, sliding and laughing harder than I have in years.

Of course when it comes to grandchildren, we have to be cognizant not only of our own boundaries, but also of those of our grandchildren's parents. From the beginning, I understood that respecting the wishes of my sons and their spouses, and following their instructions related to their children's diet and bedtime, were essential. Sometimes I see friends attempting to correct parenting mistakes they believe their children are making. This is not our job. As grandparents, our role is to love and support both our children and their children—not to push them into accepting wisdom we may feel we learned the hard way and wish to share.

In the rare instances when I disagree with my children's parenting approach, I hold my tongue and keep the big picture in mind. And that big picture is my relationship with them and their families. My goal is to have an excellent, long-term relationship based on trust. When that relationship is solid, I can have all the fun with my grandchildren that I want (in truth, I can never have enough).

When my first grandchild was born, I remember holding him in my arms and feeling a sweeping love I had never experienced before—but I have felt it since at the birth of each successive grandchild. With them, I have a chance to do things better and right. My love for my grandchildren keeps me young and vibrant and filled with purpose. That sort of unconditional love gives us what all beautiful, enduring relationships do: gratitude, joy, and a compelling reason to be our very best and enrich the world as much as we can.

CHAPTER 5

LOVE (AND SEX) OVER 50

Take ownership of your desire.

Ah, sweet romance. There was a time when my life was defined by romantic relationships. Being in love, finding love, keeping love or leaving love was a central, shaping force in my life, determining where I lived, what I did, how I saw my future. That time has passed. I have been a single woman for fifteen years, and I thoroughly enjoy my unattached life, 80 percent of the time. I am free to travel when and where I want; the only dirty dishes I have to wash are, for the most part, my own. But there are days when I yearn for the tenderness of marriage and the warmth of romantic companionship.

As women get older, we are more and more likely to be alone, whether as a result of divorce or widowhood, or simply because we have chosen to forgo a romantic relationship. While some of my friends are in stable and loving relationships, many are single, like me. And those who are on their own often admit to feeling as I do—mostly happy, occasionally lonely. But there is a larger, more important desire that eclipses both our occasional loneliness and even the pleasure we take in solitude.

What do women *really* want after the children have grown? We want freedom and self-determination, suggests Deirdre Bair in her book *Calling It Quits: Late-Life Divorce and Starting Over.* Bair conducted in-depth interviews with 184 women and 126 men who had divorced after three, four or even five decades of marriage. Freedom and the desire for control over their rest of their lives emerged as consistent themes. Another recurring theme: the notion that older adulthood is "my time"—and must be used now or lost forever. "No matter how comfortably situated they are, how lovely their home and successful their children, they divorce because they cannot go on living in the same old rut with the same old person," Bair wrote in a 2010 essay for *The New York Times.* Indeed, the desire for freedom and control has been a recurring theme expressed by many of the women interviewed for this book. Many of us feel that we are entering a golden age of sorts; the insecurities that may have shaped our younger selves have begun to melt away and we feel ready to begin a new and confident chapter. In some cases, that means leaving our husbands behind.

Grey Divorce

When Fried Kemper and I divorced in 2008, I didn't realize that I was part of a growing trend: grey divorce. Couples over 50 have one of the highest divorce rates, and two-thirds of those splits are instigated by women, says a 2004 AARP study of more than 1,100 people. Women in the study cited physical and emotional abuse, infidelity and drug use as reasons for leaving their marriages, but they also spoke about unhappiness, boredom, loneliness and poor communication.

None of these reasons for divorce are necessarily new: some are as old as the hills. But a number of factors have spurred the higher divorce rates in older couples.

While older women are particularly vulnerable to poverty, we are more financially self-sufficient than women of our mothers' generation. This relative financial health, combined with our growing longevity and the loss of stigma around divorce, are all making it easier than ever for women to simply walk away. Gone are the days when we stayed in a marriage because we felt we had no choice. Today, many women can leave, and so they do.

"Women may feel like they've gotten to a point where they feel they have endured a less than satisfactory marriage," says Resa Eisen. They have "put their time in" caring for children, perhaps supporting their spouse's career and focusing on the needs and wants of others. And as they enter their third act, profound life changes can prompt these women to decide they have had enough. It may be that the children have grown up and become established in their own lives. In fact, the feared impact of a divorce on children is by far the main reason people take so long to divorce, even when the children are grown, according to the AARP report. The death of a closed loved one—especially a parent—can also cause women to question seriously how they are living their lives, and prompt discussions or thinking around divorce, Eisen says.

"The response is often, 'I need to be out of this.' . . . The solution to the problem of an unhappy marriage is to get rid of the problem altogether."

According to the AARP study, one in four older men are blindsided by the divorce, even though their wives may have been considering divorce for a decade or longer. One key difference, discovered by Neil Chethik, author of *VoiceMale: What Husbands Really Think about Their Marriages, Their Wives, Sex, Housework, and Commitment,* is that women seem to have a lower unhappiness threshold than their partners. In his book, Chethik suggests that, unlike many men, women want their marriages to be "very good," not just sufficiently good. A 2013 Revera study of more than one thousand Canadians found that adults over age 66 often feel optimistic about aging, with an overall sense that the best is yet to come. When women don't feel their marriage will give them that "best life" they crave, it makes sense that they may want to end it.

While some divorces come to fruition, many more are threatened, discussed, explored and ultimately dropped. While researching *Calling It Quits,* Bair explains that she was surprised by the number of couples who were "divorced while married." They lived under the same roof and were legally married, but they ate alone, had their own bedrooms and lived largely separate lives.

Eisen has seen women in her practice who "raise the divorce card" as a way to underscore to their partners the depths of their displeasure with their marriage, in the hopes of initiating communication, therapy or a deeper investigation of the underlying problems in the marriage. In this way, raising the issue of divorce is sometimes less a signal that the relationship is over than a cry for help.

Rethinking Divorce

I understand the desire to free oneself of marriage. When I look back on my decision to leave Pierre, I have sadness, but no regrets. As much as we loved each other, our marriage was ill-fated, because of the difference in our ages, our temperaments and our expectations of family life. But my marriage to Fried was a different story. I gave my heart and soul to that man. It is one of the greatest regrets of my life that my mental illness contributed to my inability to fight for my marriage. At the time I was broken by grief after the death of my son and believed I needed to be alone. Perhaps this was true. But sometimes I look back and feel that the freedom I so desperately wanted could have been possible within the context of that marriage, and I have missed my husband's love.

In truth, it wasn't only my mental illness that contributed to the breakdown of my second marriage. At the time, I was bored with my life. The children were older and I was capable of doing and contributing more. But I was secure, and Fried's business provided us with a wonderful, comfortable life. He was generous and would have supported me doing anything I wanted. It was I who needed to get my life going, and I was having a difficult time giving myself the push.

I remember one evening driving my son Kyle to a party way out in the country. He and I were arguing over something. He looked at me with all the irritation a teenager can muster (which is significant) and said, "Mom, get a life." Millions of mothers around the world have heard this very thing. I'm sure I'd heard it before. But this night, his words absolutely infuriated me. He struck a nerve, and he had a point. I was bored and waiting for others to give me a life. But I was the only person who could give myself that. I wish I had taken Kyle's advice sooner.

Still, as much as I have come to embrace my solitude, there is a bone-deep part of me that feels people are meant to be paired. When I observe my friends who have happy, solid marriages, I experience a profound yearning for intimate companionship. And while I know that some people find long-lasting love in their sixties and seventies, I'm not sure I can go there anymore. Let's face it, I am older, and the men who interest me are older too. With Pierre and with Fried, I was more than prepared to age together. But to be perfectly frank about it, I don't want to be anyone's nurse. So here I sit, wrapped up in a romantic conundrum: I yearn for intimate companionship, but I have no interest in younger men, nor do I wish to take on the challenges of a new relationship with an older man.

So when my friends discuss marriage with me and talk about the possibility of leaving their husbands, the counsel I provide is to tread carefully and think it through. The love that is realized in a long and fruitful marriage doesn't happen overnight and isn't something to be casually discarded. The truth is that, when you divorce in older adulthood, you can end up dreadfully alone. You lose not only your partner, but also a huge part of your family. I adored Fried's family. After we split, these special people vanished from my life. I felt their absence profoundly.

My beliefs around fighting for one's marriage are so strong that I don't even believe that infidelity—either one's partner's or one's own—should be an automatic reason to divorce or otherwise leave a long-term relationship. I have heard extramarital sex described as the "ultimate betrayal." Really? Sex is a basic instinct, and sexual attraction can be incredibly powerful. I remember the first time I met Teddy Kennedy. We were at a state dinner in New York. I would later come to know him as a very kind, thoughtful person. But that evening, I felt such a pull toward him that we couldn't even stand within a couple of metres of one another. Pierre was not amused.

I am not condoning affairs by any means. But again, when it comes to breaking up a marriage, I say proceed with caution. The alternative may not be as rosy as it seems.

The idea of exploring freedom and personal wants and desires within a marriage *before* leaving it is a recurring theme in Eisen's practice when she counsels women or couples who are considering divorce. "The problem for men and women at this stage of life is that the fantasy of what their lives are going to be like once they've divorced is often not the reality."

Life after divorce is often far less comfortable and financially secure, for starters. As we learn in Chapter 8 (Watch Your Money, Honey), a woman's standard of living is often cut in half after she divorces. University of British Columbia professor Deborah O'Connor divorced her husband at age 50. Five years later, she was still embroiled in a legal battle that had cost her an estimated $150,000 in legal fees. "It did me in," O'Connor told *The Globe and Mail* in 2012.

But money isn't the only challenge. The AARP study found that a third of people who divorce later in life suffer from loneliness or depression. One-quarter endure feelings of betrayal, failure and feeling unloved. One-fifth experience feelings of inadequacy. "Women who leave their marriages at this point of precipitously thinking that divorce is the solution can end up in a place where they're much more lonely and uncertain about what the future's going to be," says Eisen.

She stresses that the potential for uncertainty or loneliness doesn't mean that divorce isn't the right move for certain couples, but simply that it's important for women to fully explore their options before exiting a long-standing marriage.

Eisen urges women to reflect first upon what they feel is missing: Excitement? Adventure? Companionship? Dissatisfaction is often experienced as a cavernous, gnawing feeling, but she says women need to decide what, specifically, they want more of in their lives.

Vancouver-based family, marriage and sex therapist Dr. Bianca Rucker has counselled couples who present with a variety of challenges. But one issue crops up more than others. "Women want to be listened to," she says. "They want to be heard."

Therapy is an excellent way to facilitate being heard, at least in my experience. And while it's certainly far more common— and accepted—to seek therapy today than it was even a decade ago, it still surprises me how many people navigate life's crises *without* seeking professional help. When it comes to divorce, says Eisen, "it's so much better to make an informed decision than a reactive one." Talking through your situation with your partner in front of a trained therapist is one way for both of you to air your grievances. "If a woman agrees to have counselling with her husband, it becomes a process of discovering whether the marriage will work or whether it won't." Therapy can help a couple jointly arrive at a conclusion about the future of their marriage. "It's very different than if one person simply leaves the other person—especially if one of the partners wants to remain married."

Just as critical as having your partner hear you is actually hearing *yourself* and then taking responsibility for creating the experiences and feelings you most desire, says Eisen. She relates a story about a client who was very unhappy in her marriage; she was worn out from constantly having to cook and clean the home and fed up over a lack of romance. She wanted out. Eisen urged the woman to imagine what her life would be like if she were to simply go out to a movie, attend a lecture she wanted to hear or otherwise fulfill her desire to be off the hook. The woman felt it "would never fly." She did not believe she could actually let go of her caregiving role within the context of her marriage. But the reality, Eisen explains, is paradoxical. "What I find is when women start to step out and do things that they really want and need to do, husbands often follow."

Eisen and her client started by focusing on one main unfulfilled desire: the woman's craving for more romance. Together, they made a plan that, in order to fulfill her desire for more romance in the relationship, *she* would start organizing weekly dates, rather than waiting around in the vain hope that her husband would do so. She selected the activity, she hired a nurse to stay with her aging mother and she asked her husband out. Her husband's response: pure appreciation. "It wasn't that he didn't want to go out on dates—he just never found the time to arrange them." After several dates, the husband surprised the woman by arranging one himself and finding someone to stay home with his mother-in-law. Over time, he began planning more and more romantic outings for her.

"We can get stuck in this funny little dynamic that we can never shift from this role we've fallen into in our relationships," Eisen says. "But when we own our desires and step out of that role, our partners often follow." And when our partners don't follow? That's a good clue that the marriage is in trouble, she says.

If you're in a relationship where you feel unfulfilled, Eisen suggests, pose yourself a series of questions. What do you desire? Are you willing to take ownership of your desire? How will you take action?

Some marriages, like mine to Pierre, for instance, are simply not meant to last. But Eisen—as did my son Kyle in his own way ("Get a life")—raises a significant point: neither marriage nor divorce will fulfill us if we don't first take responsibility for making ourselves happy.

Finding Love

The AARP study found that older divorced women who wanted a relationship usually found a new one within two years of their divorce. Which perhaps goes to show that as much as we crave our freedom, the lure of romance never completely fades. Just where are these older women finding partners? Often they are introduced through mutual friends and acquaintances. But more and more older adults are connecting over the Internet.

The world of online dating is foreign to me, although I do have a giggle when I consider how my online profile might read: *Twice-divorced mother of five and grandmother to seven with a colourful past seeks a new man in her life. Must not behave in any way old or like a "fuddy duddy," though must be age-appropriate. I am no cougar.* A Google search of online dating sites for older women yields many results. In fact, dating experts, such as *Huffington Post* columnist Lisa Copeland, say that online dating is the easiest way to meet single men over 50. I find this a comforting form of insurance, because much as I enjoy my single life, I have made forays into dating and these attempts have been trying.

A while back I met a distinguished man at a dinner party given by a mutual friend. He was tall, handsome in a craggy sort of way and elegantly dressed. We hit it off immediately. For a few days, my hopes soared. It took only a single date to realize that they were unfounded. He was—how do I put this nicely?—an arrogant snob. While this story gives me a good chuckle, it underscores a rather sticky problem: despite the more promising stories we hear of couples finding true love after age 60, romance in older adulthood is hard to find. Moreover, it has its pitfalls.

There is, for one thing, the challenge of exes and stepchildren. Calista married a well-off man later in life and is now treated with suspicion and often disrespect by his grown children, who wrongly believe she was only after him for his money. And then there are women who do have money who can become prey to men who want, as one friend puts it, "a nurse or a purse, or a nurse *and* a purse." Further complicating matters is that older women will often enter relationships with older men.

It took Ann White years to work through the grief of losing the love of her life to cancer. She eventually sold the home they had lived in together, purchased a new car and took up gardening again. When her family and friends sensed she was ready to move on, her cousin introduced her to a gentleman friend. They dated briefly and discovered a shared love for real estate. He had some rental properties, and she was a former kitchen designer who loved nothing more than finding unique properties and beautifying them. They decided to go splits on a new property as an investment. As their relationship deepened, they decided to move into their investment property together. But shortly after they moved in, the trouble started. Her partner—gallant and considerate before they shared an address—lost his appetite for helping with household chores. Where once they had cooked together and enjoyed relaxed meals, now he sat in front of the television while Ann cooked. He would stay there for the rest of the night, pushing Ann—who enjoys quiet evenings—into a little study at the back of the house. Ann was soon ready to end her relationship with the man, but as she was preparing herself for that conversation, he had a heart attack. Since he had no family or friends nearby, Ann felt obliged to look after him until he was healthy enough to be independent once again. Now Ann has returned to her single life in the city, wiser but poorer from her attempt to integrate her life with another's.

Like many women of her generation—Ann is in her late sixties—she was raised with the expectation that she would take care of the housekeeping duties. As a younger woman raising children, it was a role she happily fulfilled. But after her children left the house and in the years Ann spent on her own following the death of her husband, she came to relish the freedom and independence of the single life. "I learned to love making my own decisions about how to arrange the furniture, what to cook and when, what colour to paint the walls, whether I was going to sleep in or not. I don't like having to consult." Finding a new relationship satisfied her need for companionship, but it also threw her back into a caretaker role—one she is determined not to take on again.

"I certainly feel that I would never choose an older man again—someone whom I may eventually have to nurse." In discussions with her happily married friends, Ann says many of them have concluded that while they are committed to their relationships and to standing beside their husbands no matter what, "if they lost their partners, they'd likely not attach themselves again." Freedom is not an easy thing to give up—especially for a new relationship with an older man who may imminently require round-the-clock care.

Dr. Rucker, a registered marriage, family and sex therapist, has seen a compelling option among her clientele: women find someone they trust with whom they have sex casually on an as-desired basis.

The ideal solution, in my mind, would be to once again find a man who covets his freedom as much as I always have. While men have traditionally had a reputation as lovers of casual sex, in my experience, men are as likely as women to want sex to lead to a long-term commitment. The only man I ever dated who enjoyed freedom as much as I did was Jack Nicholson. He was a wonder-ful, funny, truly free man. He understood that marriage and mon-ogamy were simply not ideally suited to his life as a movie star. How I loved my time with him. Sometimes I feel what I need is a seventy-year-old financially independent snowboarder. Someone who is hunky, solvent, adventure-loving and happy to enjoy the comforts of the body, but also the freedom of solitude. Is this a fantasy? Perhaps. But I will continue looking.

Which brings me to my next topic.

Sex after 60

As we age, and especially after menopause, there can be a gradual lessening of libido. But this doesn't mean the libido disappears. Far from it. In fact, Dr. Rucker has found that in some cases, new or established couples may have even more sex after the age of 60 than they did when they were in their thirties and forties. "People have more time for each other and for sex," she says. "There is the overriding sense of 'Now it's our turn.'"

And while libido may lessen, the desire for sex is complex and multifaceted, she says. Sexual desire is really made up of three parts: the biological urge, the chemistry or attraction between partners, and your own erotic frame of mind. While the biological urge may decrease over time, strong chemistry or a better understanding of how to lull yourself into an erotic frame of mind can all promote a desire for sex, no matter how old you are, says Dr. Rucker.

Of course, there are challenges in post-60 sex. Both men and women tend to want and need more foreplay than they did when they were younger. And because of various age-related physical challenges, such as, say, arthritis, sex may be uncomfortable. Men may have more trouble getting and maintaining an erection. And for women, vaginal dryness can become a challenge to intercourse.

Dr. Jennifer Pearlman, a physician and the founder of Toronto-based women's clinic Ageless Vitality, is very matter-of-fact on the subject: "Maintaining a healthy vagina is the key to your sexual future." After menopause, she says, the vagina changes—it shrinks, becomes paler and loses sensitivity. As the vagina changes anatomically, women may experience discomfort during sex, or may be more prone to vaginal or urinary tract infections, she says. And while drugs like Viagra have helped older men get into and stay in the mood, the combination of a Viagra-treated man and a post-menopausal woman with a dry, shrunken vagina isn't a good one. In Dr. Pearlman's practice, she often treats women who, after not having had sex with their partners for months or even years, experience vaginal pain or even injury after their husbands have been prescribed a drug like Viagra.

Ensuring the vagina is properly lubricated is an important first step, something that Dr. Pearlman helps some of her patients accomplish with low doses of local estrogen. She also notes that libido is connected to brain health, how women feel about themselves, sleep, mood, body image and stress. Healthy sex requires that all parts work together.

Dr. Rucker has found that the older women who enjoy sex the most are those who take good care of themselves, are committed to sound health, and who happily accept themselves and their bodies, including changes over time.

Both Dr. Rucker and Dr. Pearlman note that new partners often do wonders for libido, but there are steps that women can take to enhance their sexual relationships, especially in long-standing relationships that have become a little stale. In a workshop she delivers about sex after age 60, Dr. Rucker offers women a number of tips to enhance their intimate lives. She encourages women to carve out time for themselves each day to connect with their partners by talking, kissing and cuddling. Taking time to consider what you most value about sex—be it adventurousness or close physical touch—can help you understand and ask for the things you most want. Being as active as possible during sex promotes enjoyment, as does stretching your comfort zone and trying new or different things. To put yourself in an erotic frame of mind, recall a peak sexual experience with your partner, and then work backward to remember just what put you in the mood. This can help you recreate similar circumstances in order to put you in an erotic frame of mind once again.

Most important, paying attention to the unmet yearnings in your life, sexual or otherwise, is the first step toward finding ways to satisfy them.

Beauty: Be Your "Real Self"
It is difficult to talk about romance—especially new romance—without talking about beauty. And this is where crone-hood can be especially challenging. Because we are no longer maidens. Our bodies change and our beauty changes as well. What we gain in wisdom and experience, we lose in other aspects. The English-Canadian actress Kim Cattrall, known for her portrayal

of sex-bomb Samantha in the TV series *Sex and the City* is now starring in a new show, *Sensitive Skin*, about a woman in mid-life confronting the issues we're looking at in this book. In an interview on *George Stroumboulopoulos Tonight* in 2014, she discussed the enormous pressure on women to remain beautiful as they age. On the one hand, she said, we scorn women for using Botox and plastic surgery to keep a youthful appearance. On the other hand, we ridicule them for turning into "old hags." She described the pain she felt after a close-up photo of her fifty-year-old knee was plastered across a magazine.

So what do we do? Age gracefully—that is, without the help of dyes and fillers—or fight it tooth and nail? For actresses like Cattrall—and indeed, for many women who feel a need to remain youthful in a modern working environment—maintaining beauty is an unspoken imperative.

When I was doing interviews and publicity tours for *Changing My Mind*, I dyed my hair blond because I wanted to cover up my greys with as little maintenance as possible. The day I went back to my natural reddish-brown, I remember having lunch with Sacha. "You didn't notice my hair," I said, after we'd finished our meal and he'd said nothing. "Of course I haven't said anything. You're back to looking like your real self," he said.

Ah, our "real selves." Now that is a loaded identity. I use soft bulbs in my bathroom lights for the simple reason that I don't want to spend too much time looking at myself. The so-called real me has wrinkles and, were I to quit my beauty regime altogether, greyish-white hair. I don't enjoy seeing myself this way, so I colour my hair and put on makeup when I go out. I try to look my best, and at this point in my life, looking my best necessitates some artfulness. Does this mean I'm not being the "real me"? I hardly think so.

I have not yet resorted to Botox, though I do not judge women who have. There is so much politicization of women's looks and choices. The last thing we need is more judgment. My feeling is that once you start with Botox, you simply must keep going; otherwise your investment is lost. So it becomes a trap.

And yet, the loss of youthful beauty can be hard to bear. From a beauty perspective, as we lose estrogen, we lose bone density, muscle and collagen. "We lose some of the structure to our face," says Dr. Pearlman. And it is this loss of facial volume that causes the skin to sag, jowls to appear and wrinkles to form. Years ago the solution was plastic surgery. And if you are an interventionist sort of person you may still have surgery, but you will more likely go the injectables route first, whether it be Botox or fillers. Both are approved for therapeutic use, and try as I might I have not found conclusive studies showing long-term ill effects of either. And yet, I cannot help but fear that injecting foreign substances into the skin—Botox in particular—is tempting fate. Some of us will refuse to intervene, be it by scalpel or needle. But increasing numbers of women are opting for an injectable of some kind. And as Dr. Pearlman points out, the risks associated with fillers are far lower than the risks associated with a facelift.

If, like me, you want to stay away from both, there are other options to improve the complexion, including laser treatments to help even out skin pigmentation or tighten the skin.

For the most part, I am an advocate of aging honestly. I feel the pull to maintain my looks for as long as possible, but I don't want to go to extreme measures. My grandchildren tell me I am all "cracked," and I delight in this. Justin defended my wrinkles by telling the children "it is because Gramma has laughed most of her life." He did not mention that I have also cried a lot; those lines are etched deep. I want to look like the British actress Maggie Smith—lined and beautiful, each wrinkle a testament to my years on earth.

Good grooming goes a long way. A friend of mine stays chic by maintaining a uniform: good jeans, a crisp white shirt and a beautiful Hermès scarf knotted around her neck. I have always admired what I know to be the French approach to good grooming: purchasing a quality suit once per year whose parts can be worn together or separately on an almost daily basis. For older adults, well-structured pieces hold their shape—and ours—so much better.

I have tried to instruct my daughter in the art of French dressing: investing occasionally in good pieces, versus buying cheaper clothing in volume. I am making some headway, and this is good enough. I cannot worry too much about other people anymore. It will give me wrinkles. Far better to worry about myself—or perhaps try not to worry at all.

CHAPTER 6

THE BALANCING ACT:
SLEEP, NUTRITION AND EXERCISE

Do everything you can to avoid going "gentle into that good night."

Happiness, fulfillment, adventure, purpose and joy—all the things that make our lives wonderful and worth living—hinge on sound health. When I was a younger woman and brimming with the bounce-back factor, I took my health for granted. Staying up late and eating too much sugar hardly bothered me. But since crossing the threshold of my sixties, I've noticed that my body requires much more TLC than it once did. As I have endured my own health problems and watched friends deal with serious diagnoses such as Type 2 diabetes, heart disease and breast cancer, the foundational triad of excellent health— restorative sleep, nourishing nutrition and exercise—has taken on new significance. I am in good health now, but what can I do to prolong it?

"After age 60, the burden of chronic disease sets in," says Dr. Jennifer Pearlman, the willowy, gravitas-filled physician and founder of Ageless Vitality, a Toronto-based practice devoted to helping women age well. While Dr. Pearlman treats women of all ages, it's the post-60 crowd who come to her with a "basket of symptoms and conditions"—ranging from turkey neck and sleeplessness to heart disease, diabetes and osteoporosis. When I look at my friends who are ten or fifteen years ahead of me, I see many who get around with walking aids, live with some sort of chronic disease and take multiple medications.

The health problems we experience as we age restrict the scope of our lives. Getting around is harder when we have a cane or walker, so we are tempted to stay at home. To be spared the occasional embarrassment of urinary incontinence, we might avoid socializing because we really might laugh so hard we pee our pants. (Less entertaining in practice than in theory, it turns out.)

If the body really is a vessel for the soul, than the health fears (or expectations?) our society has traditionally held about aging— that most of us will eventually become old, sick and infirm—necessarily equate to smaller, more subdued and restricted lives. And this is precisely the opposite of what I—indeed, most of us—want.

But if the fulfillment and vibrancy of the last third of our lives depend so much on health, and physical decline is a part of aging, what can we do to make a difference? The answer, according to health experts, is *everything*. We must do everything we can to not go gently into that good night.

In my case, it's been time to "age proactively" for a good fifteen years. Montreal-based physician and geriatrician Dr. Cara

Tannenbaum, who specializes in older women's health, says the window of opportunity to begin shaping a healthy old age truly opens by around age 50. By the mid-sixties, if you haven't taken a good, hard look at your lifestyle, well, you should. Or, as Dr. Pearlman puts it, "Leave the aging gracefully to your grandmothers. It's time to age proactively." Of course, you couldn't be blamed for buying into the "aging gracefully" mantra. In this, as in so many aspects of our lives, we cannot truly look to our mothers for guidance. Had I asked my own mother, at age 60, what *she* was doing to "age proactively," she would have laughed out loud.

It's not that our mothers and grandmothers weren't as bothered by achy knees and chronic disease as we are. But the last decade has seen huge advances in the understanding and treatment of aging-related illness and decline. Thanks to advances in the field of epigenetics, we now understand our DNA is no longer necessarily our destiny. Yes, knowing our family history is crucial in predicting the risk of diseases such as breast and ovarian cancer. But regardless of our genes, there is in fact a tremendous amount we can do to stave off physical decline and preserve our health for as long as possible. And that's the key, really—preserving health for *as long as possible.*

If, like me, you've reached 65, chances are decent that you are in for a long life—if you're a woman. According to Statistics Canada, 50 percent of women who live to be 65 are likely to live past the age of 85. (At which point there will be 2.5 women for every man, which may be a good or bad thing, depending on one's view.) But as geriatricians warn, it's one thing to have a twenty-year life expectancy; it's quite another to have a *healthy* life expectancy. I don't want to spend the next twenty years merely living. I want to be travelling, seeking adventure, basking in the sunshine, taking walks, going to plays, chasing my grandchildren and generally enjoying myself. I expect you do too.

To realize this dream, we'll have to ensure we have the physical health to underwrite it. And that means dropping the laissez-faire attitude toward health that we held in our younger years, and cultivating a health-oriented mindset.

The Bad News

I prefer to ignore or bury bad news for as long as possible. However, in the spirit of change, renewal and general self-improvement, I'll deal with the unpleasantness first. As we age, we face a host of threats to our health. This isn't earth-shattering, of course. I don't know of a single woman my age who doesn't have *some* sort of health complaint. Except, perhaps, for my friend Dotty, who teaches bootcamp, has a formidable ability to resist sugar and still has the body of a 35-year-old. Dotty notwithstanding, the rest of us have some sort of health complaint we didn't have five years ago.

The body has a stunning capacity to develop a myriad of weird, not-wonderful diseases, injuries and complications, but some are too common to ignore. They are the Geriatric Giants, which I list here, in random order: chronic disease, urinary incontinence, falls and polypharmacy. (Another common health concern in aging is cognitive impairment. We'll discuss that topic at length in Chapter 7.) In the section that follows, we'll look at these challenges—along with some others that you may not yet have considered. Brace yourself. The next section is a little like back labour; it will get worse before it gets better.

CHRONIC DISEASE

Chronic diseases such as cancer, heart disease, stroke and diabetes are estimated by the World Health Organization to kill 36 million people worldwide each year. Treating these chronic diseases soaks up roughly three-quarters of health care spending in the United States. And these scary numbers promise to get worse as our population ages. One in nine women will be diagnosed with breast cancer (the most common cancer for women) over the course of her life, and more than half of all those cases affect women ages 50 to 69, says Katarina Gagne of the Breast Cancer Society of Canada. And while screening and early detection have helped to reduce death rates from breast cancer to record lows— the five-year survival rate is now 88 percent—the numbers are still grim. Sixty-five Canadian women are diagnosed with breast cancer each day, and fourteen die from the disease each day.

I have watched many friends battle cancer, and have experienced the sense of powerlessness we all feel when we, or someone we love, is struck with the disease. It is true that some of the risk factors for breast cancer are outside our locus of control. For instance, simply being a woman over age 50 increases your risk. Being born with "dense breast tissue"—or heavy breasts—can increase your risk factor as well because lumps are often harder to detect in dense breasts. And finally, there is a genetic component. But even here, the reminder that our DNA is not our destiny is worth heeding. In 2013, the actress Angelina Jolie made headlines with her decision to undergo a double mastectomy after discovering she had the BRCA1 gene. Jolie's mother died of breast cancer at age 56, and in an op-ed for *The New York Times*, Jolie stated her own doctors had told her she had an 87 percent risk for developing breast cancer and a 50 percent risk of developing ovarian cancer. Jolie assessed her odds and opted for surgery—a proactive approach that would have been unheard of a few decades ago. Her decision is an excellent example of how research can revolutionize the battle against chronic illnesses such as breast cancer. Much more is needed.

There are many other risk factors for breast cancer that fall well within our locus of control. Breakthrough research from the American Cancer Society that followed 73,000 post-menopausal women over seventeen years found in 2013 that an hour of vigorous walking per day reduces a woman's risk of developing breast cancer by 25 percent. Controlling body weight and eating a balanced diet also help. (Indeed, diet and exercise are crucial in preventing all sorts of ills, as we explore later in this chapter.)

But as scary as the *C* word is for us, it may not be the most deadly of all the chronic diseases. According to 2008 data from Statistics Canada, that distinct honour goes to cardiovascular disease (i.e., heart disease and stroke), which is the number-one killer of women. When I heard this, I was surprised. Like many people, I've long associated heart disease with men—round-bellied, red-faced men with high blood pressure. But in fact, across much of the developed world, more women die of cardiovascular disease each year than men. Dr. Beth Abramson, a cardiologist and spokesperson for the Heart and Stroke Foundation, points out that while death rates from cardiovascular illness have decreased in men since the 1970s, more women are dying from heart disease than ever before. In part, this is because the population is aging.

Women enjoy some protection from heart disease before menopause. Estrogen is believed to regulate cholesterol in the body and dilate the arteries. But as estrogen levels drop after menopause, a woman's risk for heart disease increases significantly. The trouble is, women are often the last to know. A survey from the Heart and Stroke Foundation found that only one in eight women surveyed understood that cardiovascular disease was her most serious health concern, and only one in three knew it was the leading cause of death.

Physicians suggest that women often under-report heart attack symptoms such as pressure in the chest, pain in the left arm, neck, jaw, shoulder or upper back, or abdominal discomfort; shortness of breath; right arm pain; nausea or vomiting; sweating; light-headedness or dizziness; and unusual fatigue. Because of this tendency, by the time women do show up in emergency rooms, heart damage may already have occurred.

In her book *Heart Health for Canadians: The Definitive Guide,* Dr. Abramson tells two patient stories that demonstrate just how lethal second-guessing symptoms can be. In one case, a 44-year-old woman with a family history of heart disease woke up in the middle of the night with heaviness in her chest. Her husband called 911, and when they arrived at the hospital, doctors discovered she'd had a heart attack. She was immediately treated and because she had acted without hesitation, she did not sustain any irreparable muscle damage to her heart.

Compare this experience to that of a busy 64-year-old woman

who began feeling ill with nausea and severe indigestion in the lead-up to a major fundraiser she was planning. Halfway through the event she became so ill she had to go home to bed. Over the next three days she and her husband debated whether or not she should go to the hospital. When she did finally arrive at the ER, she had already suffered moderate damage to her heart, and she will never make a full recovery. Dr. Abramson suggests this "second guess" mindset could be partially to blame for the fact that women are more likely to die following a heart attack or stroke than a man. If you are experiencing symptoms of a heart attack, override your self-doubt and get thee to an emergency room, and prepare to kick up a fuss if you are told to go home and take a baby Aspirin. Not only do women under-report their symptoms, but also they are often under-treated within the health care system.

As Dr. Abramson reports in her book, women are not as likely as men to be treated by a cardiologist, and if they are treated at a smaller hospital, they are less likely to be transferred to a facility with a specialty cardiac care unit. Though these care gaps are diminishing, Dr. Abramson urges women to advocate on their own behalf. If you are presenting with symptoms of a heart attack, ask these questions: Could it be my heart? Do I need an angiogram or other test? Should I see a specialist? They may spur health workers to give you the care you need.

By the time you do have symptoms of heart disease, of course, the proverbial ship has sailed. Yes, many women do recover and change their lifestyles for the better. But wouldn't it be best to avoid it in the first place? This is where understanding your risk factors can help.

Diabetes, smoking and a lack of physical activity can all increase your chances of cardiovascular disease. Metabolic syndrome—a worrying cocktail of belly fat, high blood pressure and blood sugar, and bad cholesterol—puts you at risk as well. Mental stress and depression—both of which are more common in women than in men—put increased stress on the heart, as do lower levels of estrogen. But while natural estrogen protects against heart disease, Dr. Abramson warns that hormone replacement therapy (HRT) is *not* the magic bullet. In fact, she points to studies that have linked HRT with increased risk of breast cancer, heart attack and stroke. It's worth pointing out, however, that physicians are divided on its risks.

If you, like me, have any of the risk factors or symptoms I've just mentioned, talk to your doctor and ask the questions Dr. Abramson suggests. We explore later in this chapter steps you can take to eradicate the risk factors before they become a problem.

URINARY INCONTINENCE

The gifts of pregnancy, childbirth and menopause combine to make us twice as likely as men to experience urinary incontinence. Menopause and the resulting drop in estrogen and testosterone (yes, women have testosterone as well) reduce muscle mass significantly and shorten the urethral sphincter, causing it to stop closing properly. This, combined with weight gain, which puts pressure on the bladder, can cause urinary incontinence. The condition affects millions of women, as evidenced by the plethora of pads available in any drugstore. For some women, the problem is little more than an inconvenience. For others, it can be debilitating and prevent them from going out in public for fear of humiliation. Kegel exercises are a huge help. You know, those exercises we were instructed to do to prepare for labour but invariably neglected or forgot until a few days before our babies' due dates? Yes, those Kegels. Strengthening the pelvic muscles is the best remedy for urinary incontinence. Surgery is another option for more serious cases.

Dr. Tannenbaum says she has seen women suffer for years before seeking treatment because they believe incontinence is an inevitable part of aging. "It absolutely is not," she says. In fact, she warns against automatically accepting *anything* as a normal part of aging.

FALLS

When my grandchildren come to my condo for the weekend, I watch them fall dozens of times a day. Occasionally, one of them will have a cry-worthy tumble, but for the most part, they barely notice when they trip. Ah, the good old days. The older we get, the harder we fall.

According to the U.S. Centers for Disease Control, falls in older adults (both men and women) are the leading cause of fatal and non-fatal injuries, including traumatic brain injuries. Rates of fall-related fractures are twice as high for women as for men. This is partly explained by our relative lack of bone mineral density.

And when we are talking about a reduction in bone density and related bone fractures, we have to talk about osteoporosis. According to Osteoporosis Canada, fractures from osteoporosis are more common than heart attack, stroke and breast cancer combined. At least one in three women will suffer an osteoporotic fracture during her lifetime, and as many as 90 percent of all hip fractures are caused by osteoporosis. The problem is that older adults who fall are four to five times as likely to be admitted to a long-term facility *for a year or longer*. But even if you don't have to go and live in a treatment facility, the injuries you sustain from a fall are likely to curb your lifestyle considerably.

Diagnosis and prevention are important. Osteoporosis Canada estimates that without bone mass density (BMD) testing, 80 percent of patients with a history of fractures are not given proper therapies. Because of this, thousands of Canadians needlessly fracture their bones each year because their osteoporosis is undiagnosed and untreated. In this, as in most health concerns, it's important not only to talk to your doctor, but also to ask for a BMD test. Osteoporosis is called "the silent thief" because the reduction in bone density is usually not detected until after a fracture has already occurred. Vitamin D is also helpful in staving off the disease.

What can you do to prevent falls? Exercise—especially exercise that cultivates balance, such as tai chi—is an obvious first step. Less obvious are getting your eyes checked regularly and reducing fall hazards like rugs, little side tables and possibly even (in my case) little furry cats named Aurora who adore hanging out just outside the bedroom door. In truth, while I am committed to enhancing my balance, I have yet to get rid of my rugs. I'm working on it, though (see Chapter 9, A Home of One's Own). But Aurora is here to stay.

Closely related to falls is the general decrease in mobility we experience as we age. There are all sorts of reasons for decreased mobility—injury or illness, for instance. But one worryingly common cause is osteoarthritis. Joanne Simons, chief mission officer of the Arthritis Society, says there are currently 3 million Canadians living with osteoarthritis. "The burden is increasing," she says.

Unlike the more than ninety other forms of arthritis, many of which affect young people as well as old, osteoarthritis tends to strike older adults. The disease generally rears its head with pain or burning in the joints. And though major advances have been made in the treatment of other forms of arthritis, such as inflammatory arthritis, there's no cure for osteoarthritis—this degenerative condition gets worse each year.

The main course of treatment, says Simons, is to manage the pain and to feed the affected joints with lots of oxygen, which means movement. "It's critical to keep moving," says Simons. Unfortunately, because osteoarthritis is so painful, it's common for the afflicted to avoid moving their joints to prevent pain— which not only worsens the disease, but leads to other problems. When people stop moving and doing their normal life activities, they become more prone to depression, and Simons says there is a link between osteoarthritis and depression for this reason. Safe sports such as walking, swimming or riding a bike can all slow down osteoarthritis. To reduce your risk of developing arthritis, maintain a healthy body weight. Obesity is the leading risk factor for osteoarthritis. Losing ten pounds can remove as much as four times the force on your knees, and slow down the advance of osteoarthritis. This is key, because roughly eighty thousand people per year receive joint replacements in Canada, and across the country wait times for these surgeries are long. The joint condition often has to be especially severe in order to make it eligible for surgery. Interventions such as exercise and diet have helped people come off the surgical list altogether, says Simons.

Despite lots of research and the growing prevalence of osteoarthritis, the condition is still misunderstood, says Simon. "We constantly hear, 'My doctor said to live with it.'" She urges people to take that advice with a grain of salt. "Self-management is critical." The Arthritis Society offers a range of workshops in managing chronic pain, weight and lifestyle to help people maintain a full life as they live with the condition.

Finally, we can't very well discuss bones without discussing teeth. Oral care becomes more critical as we age. Over the last year, I've spent more time in the dentist's chair than I care to admit. And far more money than I want to think about. Root canals, implants, you name it. I have paid and suffered in the dentist's chair for it (I adore my dentist, but I really do suffer in that chair). Getting my mouth fixed is possibly the most grown-up thing I have ever done. There were far more exciting things I wanted to spend my money on. Not to mention that seeing a dentist ranks as one of the most traumatic experiences possible for me.

When I was 17, my family dentist sent me across the road to a dental surgeon for a root canal. He gave me laughing gas and then proceeded to touch me underneath my shirt. I was shaken to the core, too terrified to shout for help. When I emerged from the room, I told my mother not to pay the bill, but felt too sick to explain why. She paid the bill and we left, but I never mentioned the experience to anyone.

Years later I went to a dentist for an implant, which he performed without sedation. I remember lying in the chair, feeling the grinding of the drill in my toes. When he was finished I could barely move or speak. I didn't return to the dentist for some time. But then my teeth started cracking. A few years ago I was walking in the park with a girlfriend. I bit down on an apple and lost part of my tooth. I just knew I had to do something before they all fell out. I had horrors of a set of teeth in a glass of water by my bed. So coached myself through the process of finding a dentist I could trust.

My rationale was that it's better to have any dental work I need done now than later. In fact, Dr. Barry Dolman, a dentist and president of Ordre des dentistes du Québec, warns of the dire consequences of putting off tooth problems for a rainy day. He relates a story about a woman who complained of a problem tooth but elected to avoid treating it because it wasn't posing a huge problem at the time. A few years passed. She then had a serious heart attack and was hospitalized and put on blood thinners. Around that time, her tooth began causing her extreme discomfort and interfered with her eating. But because she could not risk going off blood thinners and was in such poor overall health, her doctors and dentist told her she could not have her problem tooth fixed. "People sometimes wonder why I'm suggesting they get a crown at age 75," says Dr. Dolman. "The reality is, they may need that tooth for another fifteen or twenty years."

As we age, we face a number of threats to our teeth. The first is a condition known as dry mouth, when saliva production is suppressed. Saliva is crucial for balancing the pH levels in the mouth and protecting teeth from decay. Combine dry mouth with the tendency for gums to recede with age and expose roots, and you have an increased risk for cavities. The solution, says Dr. Dolman, is to be aware of the types of prescribed and over-the-counter medications that cause dry mouth, including antihistamines, antidepressants, antihypertensives, sedatives and diuretics. If you are taking these medications and experiencing dry mouth, Dr. Dolman recommends speaking to both your dentist and doctor about the condition. Chewing sugar-free gum can help stimulate saliva production.

Another challenge we face as we age is that decreasing mobility or agility can actually impede our dental hygiene. Using fluoride rinses is an excellent way to give your teeth the protection they need, says Dr. Dolman. Another concern of particular relevance to older women is a condition called osteonecrosis of the jaw. This is a condition where the jawbone becomes starved of blood, weakens and begins to die. In dental patients, the condition might not present until a patient has a routine dental surgery and discovers the jawbone isn't healing properly. Dr. Dolman says that for some patients, there is a link between osteonecrosis and biophosphonates, drugs sometimes given to people suffering from osteoporosis. While osteonecrosis of the jaw is rare, Dr. Dolman says it's a serious condition. Make sure you tell your dentist about all the medications you may be taking.

POLYPHARMACY

More and more, I notice an increasing reluctance in people to take pharmaceutical drugs in favour of alternative approaches to health. While I support any choices a woman makes to be healthier, I firmly believe that pharmaceutical drugs play a major role in keeping us healthy. That said, I know that, especially for those over age 60, a confluence of health complications means that many of us have enough pharmaceuticals in our drug cabinets to restore the health of a small army. And this is precisely why polypharmacy—the use of multiple drug medications—is such a cause for concern for older adults. Certified geriatric pharmacist Carla Beaton says that a person's risks for adverse health effects increase as prescriptions are added. "The more drugs you take, the more interactions you are at risk of seeing."

According to the Agency of Healthcare Research and Quality (a division of the U.S. Department of Health and Human Services), adverse drug events result in more than 770,000 injuries and deaths *each year*.

Polypharmacy reflects an overarching theme within the health care system of adding drugs but not necessarily taking others away. Beaton explains the cycle: "You experience a health problem, so you may add one drug. This causes a side effect, so you add another drug to address the side effect, which causes something else."

It's not uncommon for polypharmacy to happen gradually, as in the scenario Beaton explains above. But there's another source of potential polypharmacy—a hospital visit to address a specific health issue. For instance, perhaps you have fallen and broken your hip. The hospital is concerned with fixing your hip and treating your pain—which is why the doctors might miss the fact that you're on thyroid medication. While you're in hospital, they stop giving you thyroid medication (it simply slips off the radar in the wake of the crisis of breaking your hip), and put you on powerful painkillers. You get out of the hospital, return home and take both your thyroid medication and the painkillers—and within a week or two you suffer an adverse drug reaction.

The best way to protect yourself from the ills of polypharmacy, Beaton says, is to meet with your pharmacist at least once per year to review all your medications. And if at any point you are prescribed another medication, meet with your pharmacist again for another review. "You want to develop a relationship with your pharmacist and see them as part of your health care team," she says.

AGE AND GENDER BIAS

Another threat we face with respect to our health is one we don't talk about nearly enough, in my opinion: bias. As much as I respect the medical system and owe a deep debt to Canadian physicians, there are ways in which the health care system is failing older women. As I pointed out in the section focused on heart disease, research has shown that women cardiac patients are less likely than men to be referred to a specialist, or to be transferred to a larger centre with a specialty cardiac unit. There are other examples of bias in the health care system, some of which I have experienced first-hand.

Earlier I mentioned the little skiing accident I had while sliding down the bunny hill with my grandson. Sacha took me to the local ER, and after three hours of nauseating pain, my shoulder was put back in its socket. I returned to Montreal and went to an orthopedic surgeon to have it checked out. He was a relatively young, self-satisfied man, who diagnosed me with an unstable shoulder. In other cases, he would recommend surgery to repair the damage, he said, but at my "advanced age," he didn't think surgery was worth it—the recovery would be slow and painful. I would simply have to live with the injury.

I went home feeling both dejected and enraged. I felt as though I had been insulted in a foreign language and lacked the ability to properly respond. Was 64 *really* too old for surgery? I was healthy, strong and had lots of energy. I didn't really believe it would take me months to recover from the surgery. But he was a doctor, and I heeded his advice. Over the next eighteen months, I dislocated the shoulder five more times. For some months after my fall, I was barely able to lift my arm. To this day, the joint can cause me aching pain. I have since spoken to other doctors who have told me that as a strong, healthy woman, I'd be an excellent candidate for shoulder surgery, despite my "advanced age."

I'm considering it, just as am I considering walking back to the hospital to find the doctor and lecture him on age and gender bias in health care, as well as the difference between chronological age and biological age. Many of the health experts interviewed for this book underlined the importance of focusing on your biological age. Some 64-year-olds may well be "too old" for shoulder surgery. I wasn't one of them, though I also know it can take two years to heal completely.

Dr. Paula Rochon, vice-president of research at Women's College Hospital in Toronto, suggests that one way to establish total equity in the health care system is to ensure women play a larger role in shaping research. "Women have not been as well represented in research," she points out. "We need to make it easier to include more gender-based studies," she says, which will build our understanding of women's unique needs and physiology.

The Good News

It's tempting to dwell on all the things that *could* go wrong with our health. But the resounding evidence is that we are in a position to be able to have a dramatic and positive influence on our overall health. And taking care of ourselves is actually quite simple. The three essential elements of health and longevity are restorative sleep, proper exercise and good nutrition.

SLEEP

Last year, after participating in a fundraiser for mental health sponsored by Shoppers Drug Mart and athletic wear retailer The Running Room, I debated with the company's founder, John Stanton, on what was the most important element of maintaining health—sleep, exercise or nutrition. He argued for exercise, and I argued for sleep. I won the debate—in my estimation, at least. Sleep is vastly important for longevity and overall health, and plays a critical role in immune function, metabolism, memory and learning. Nevertheless, the intricacies of sleep—why we need it, and what specifically happens while we are resting—remain a mystery, says sleep specialist Dr. Raymond Gottschalk, medical director of the Hamilton, Ontario–based Sleep Disorders Clinic. For instance, Dr. Gottschalk points out that the body can recuperate very well with simple rest—lying down and doing nothing. Meanwhile, sleep is a "phenomenon of reversible unconsciousness for the brain, by the brain."

The current popular "restorative sleep theory" suggests that it is the primary way our bodies restore and repair themselves. For instance, advocates maintain that a number of restorative processes, including muscle repair, tissue growth and protein synthesis, occur only when we are sleeping. Getting a good night's rest is critical for cognitive function. During our waking hours, the brain's neurons produce a by-product called adenosine. The buildup of adenosine is thought to contribute to making us feel tired. Only when we sleep does the brain have the chance to clean adenosine from our system, which is why we wake up feeling so refreshed.

Unfortunately, as essential as sleep is to our health, few women seem to be getting enough. Sleep quality frequently deteriorates after menopause, says Dr. Gottschalk. One of the reasons for this is a fragmenting of our natural sleep cycles. Every five or six minutes during sleep, the average person will "breach the surface of unconsciousness," Dr. Gottschalk says—essentially becoming more sensitive to sounds, movement or light that might wake us up. This is thought to be an evolutionary tool to protect us from predators. While teenagers require a significant sound to rouse them—more than twenty decibels in some cases—older women become much more sensitive. In addition, because estrogen is a temperature stabilizer in the body, decreases can produce hot flashes that prevent us from sleeping well.

And while older adults appear to tolerate sleep deprivation better than younger adults, research suggests that many of us are looking for solutions to frequent night-waking. Dr. Cara Tannenbaum quoted research suggesting that 30 percent of older women in Quebec, the Canadian province where I live, take sleeping pills on a regular basis. And while sleeping pills may serve as a stopgap measure for sleeplessness, they do not allow for the restorative qualities of natural sleep. What's more, because women cannot clear the medication from our systems as quickly as men, taking a sleeping pill at night can affect our ability the next day to complete activities that require one to be totally alert, like driving. Some physicians prescribe melatonin to help with sleep, but I have always preferred the old-fashioned way—sticking to a routine.

Almost every night, I follow the same pattern of activities to help my body anticipate sleep. I have a little snack. I start turning off the lights. I don't watch the news, which is too much of a downer before bed. If I watch TV it is comedy. Doing the same thing night after night helps me to anticipate sleep. I try to get exercise each day because that always helps me sleep better. And I avoid alcohol and sugar at night, both of which interrupt my sleep. Nutrition plays a tremendous role in ensuring a sound sleep, and we explore sleep-enhancing diet in the next section.

Another important consideration is the *amount* of sleep you need. While studies suggest that most people need seven to eight hours of sleep, physicians who work with older women say not to fret if you find yourself waking up after only six hours. It's common for older adults to require less sleep—especially if you are less stimulated and more sedentary than you once were. Rather than taking a sleeping pill to ensure you are getting your eight hours each night, you might consider exercising more or simply accepting that six hours of sleep is your new normal.

There are other things you can do to promote better sleep. One is to avoid screens before bed. Blue light makes us more alert and can delay melatonin production—which makes it harder for us to stay asleep. Working or doing any stimulating activity close to bedtime is also a no-no. "Sleep is a state of consciousness that is very easily influenced," says Dr. Gottschalk. Finally, because rates of sleep apnea spike in women after menopause, often because of post-menopause weight gain, controlling your weight is another important piece of the equation.

EXERCISE

I can't remember a time when I *wasn't* being advised to get lots of exercise. However, the call to get one's body moving becomes un-ignorable later in life. The benefits of exercise go far beyond feeling fit and strong. The British Women's Health and Heart Study, which has followed 2,500 women since 1999, has found that regular exercise is a key factor in reducing a woman's risk of major late-life disabilities such as frailty, heart disease and arthritis. According to the research, women who never exercise are twice as likely to develop arthritis and problems walking later in life. Exercise is crucial for maintaining a healthy body weight and maintaining the strength and stamina we need to live a full life deep into older age. But a major benefit of exercise is that it helps to reduce stress, making it an effective anti-aging tool.

And while exercise is crucial, it's not a matter of any old exercise, says Dr. Cara Tannenbaum. "A lot of people tell me, 'Oh, I'm getting enough exercise, I walk every day.' The problem is, that doesn't do anything for the muscles in your arm, or for your pelvic floor."

A well-rounded exercise regime for an older woman includes

three distinct focus areas: cardiovascular activity with agility work, strength training and balance exercises. This cardio/strength/balance trio works together to create a strong, balanced and healthy body that is more energetic, more resistant to illness and chronic joint problems such as osteoarthritis, knee and hip pain, and back problems, and less prone to falls and injury. The sooner you incorporate a well-balanced exercise program into your regime, the better.

Vancouver-based personal trainer Kate Maliha of Love Your Age Fitness specializes in exercise plans for older women. She compares two clients she works with, both of whom are in their mid-nineties. One woman—we'll call her Maria—sought out Maliha recently, after she began experiencing serious difficulties walking, which had largely kept her homebound and, because of this, diminished her socializing considerably. Given what we know about the strong link between health and community, this social isolation in turn likely suppressed her overall health even more. Contrast Maria with another client I'll call Alice. At age 95, Alice has been working with Maliha for more than fifteen years. She walks every day, and during her weekly training sessions goes through an intense combination of strength, agility and balance exercises. While Maria is housebound, Alice is continuing to work, has the stamina of a much younger woman and flies around the world delivering lectures and brushing off concerned offers for help with the stairs to the stage.

When it comes to aging and exercise, Maliha warns against allowing your *chronological* age to dictate what you can and can't do. For instance, one pervasive myth about older women and exercise is that we can't exercise *hard*. The truth is that, especially with the guidance of a professional who can help ensure you are doing exercises properly, women of all ages can work up a good sweat. The older you are, however, the more recovery time you'll need between workouts.

For this reason, women over age 50 who have some degree of urinary incontinence may have trouble with high-impact cardio-vascular exercises like running or bootcamps. In these cases, swimming, aqua-aerobics, biking or walking are all excellent alternatives. But in addition to these standard exercises, exercise specialists for older women suggest we begin integrating agility exercises into our workouts. These include ladders—the exercise popularized by football players that involves alternating high-knee steps moving forward and backward. One agility exercise Maliha uses with the 95-year-old globe-trotting Alice is a timed session in which Alice scoots around an exercise area picking up coloured balls and putting them on top of like-coloured pylons. This workout combines agility—stooping to pick things up, and avoiding stepping on the pylons—with cognitive function—matching the right balls to the right cones—all of which work together to create a longevity-enhancing workout.

Weight-bearing exercises too are critical for women over 50. Not only are we losing muscle mass, but we're losing our fast-twitch muscles more quickly than our slow-twitch muscles. Slow-twitch muscles, which are more effective in burning oxygen to produce fuel, contribute to endurance—these are what you'd use should you decide to go on a spiritual quest and hike the Camino de Santiago trail through France and Spain, for instance. Fast-twitch fibres generate lots of power quickly—these are the fibres you might use should you have to run out of a burning building. The relatively speedy die-off of fast-twitch muscles after 50 is one of the biggest contributors to the lack of "pep" that older women might experience. And what might start as a sense of general slowing down—taking our time to get in and out of the car, for instance—can transform, over time, into the shuffling walk of the aged—and a lack of both the reaction time and explosive strength you need to catch yourself after you've lost your balance. For women closer to 50, weight-bearing squats or lunges can help cultivate fast-twitch muscles. Exercises that use higher weight but lower repetitions (eight lunges with ten pounds in each hand versus fifteen lunges with five pounds per hand) can also build explosive strength.

If you haven't been on a regular weight regime in the past, Maliha recommends you seek out a trainer who specializes in working with older women before lifting heavier weights. But one simple exercise to build your power and explosiveness is simply to walk quickly up a ramp several times.

Balance work is largely preventive in your fifties and sixties, but it's common by your seventies to have fallen, had a close call that scared you or be experiencing balance problems such as difficulty standing on one leg to put your trousers on. Balance issues are often worse for women who've spent a lifetime in heels—which cause the toes to permanently curl, the calves and Achilles tendons to shorten and the foot itself to narrow. Yet it must be said there are times when a good pair of high heels is essential to a woman's well-being. I feel very sexy when I put on heels. In any case, wearing heels can significantly reduce balance and compromise ankle mobility, which increases your likelihood of tripping or injuring your ankles in older age. How do you prevent this? Aside from cutting down on heel time as much as possible, Maliha recommends balance exercises such as tai chi, gentle yoga and aqua-aerobics. Simple balance exercises you can do at home include standing in a wide stance with your legs apart and your feet directly in line with one another, so that your toes line up with the heel of your opposite foot. Once that becomes easy, try moving your gaze around, rotating your torso and even closing your eyes.

Even if we *do* manage weekly workouts targeting each of the cardio, strength and balance areas, we cannot rest on these periods of intense physical activity alone. As we get older, retire from work and cocoon in our homes, we are much more likely to lead sedentary lives. And there is a high price to pay for sitting still. Research headed by Dorothy Dunlop of Northwestern University, published in 2014, revealed that if you are 60 or over, each additional hour you spend sitting still each day doubles your risk of becoming disabled—*no matter how much you exercise.* The researchers defined disability as not being able to perform an important self-care task, such as getting dressed. So for instance, if you were to compare two 65-year-old women, one who spent twelve hours a day sitting and another who spent thirteen hours a day sitting, the thirteen-hour-a-day woman would be twice as likely to develop a disability. The study's authors came up with a number of suggestions to avoid sedentary behaviour over the course of the day: standing up when talking on the phone, parking in the farthest spot from the door when shopping to encourage walking, taking short hourly walks around the house, and using the stairs rather than the elevator, when possible.

The problem, of course, is that it can sometimes be difficult to remember just how long you have spent being sedentary. If you are up for it, there's lots of technology to help. The Fitbit—a plastic bracelet with embedded computer chips and sensors—tracks your sleep, the number of steps you take in a day, how much water you drink and how many calories you consume in a day. While something in me rebels against the idea of keeping such close tabs on myself, friends who have them swear by the rule that what is measured is usually accomplished.

NUTRITION

As a society we're more conscious of diet than ever before. Though, I think we can take dietary constraints a little too far—almost everyone seems to be allergic to something. I recently saw a funny little sign that said it all: *She's either bipolar or lactose intolerant, I can't tell which.* I had a good laugh over that. But as skeptical as I can be about the rise of self-ordained sensitivity, I am a huge proponent of the notion that food is medicine. As we age we need a good balanced diet, high in vegetables, whole grains, fruits, proteins and dairy—as much as we ever did. But there are two types of food that older women need more than ever—and that we rarely get enough of, says Dr. Jennifer Pearlman.

The first is protein. Some researchers have suggested that many dietary guidelines underestimate just how much protein older women need in order to stay in optimal health. For instance, in the United States, the recommended daily protein intake for older women is 0.36 grams for each pound of body weight. But new research suggests we need much more than that. Dr. Pearlman advises her clients to eat 90 grams of protein a day—most women are getting less than half that. It doesn't help that as we age, we usually eat less, even as our need for protein increases. Protein helps maintain muscle mass and fight off osteoarthritis-related decline as well as osteoporosis. Bottom line: eat more protein, whether you get it through lean meats, eggs, nuts, seeds or beans. Protein shakes are a simple way to boost your protein intake.

Another element our diets should include is DHA, the dietary fat found primarily in fish. DHA has an array of health benefits—it helps to nurture and preserve brain function, heart health, supple joints, a strong immune system and good eyesight. DHA protects against certain cancers and is an anti-inflammatory. And because DHA actually helps slow down cellular aging, it's a longevity booster too. This miracle oil can be found in flax, chia and hemp seeds, as well as walnuts. I love to cook fatty fish such as salmon, but doctors say it doesn't hurt to consume omega-rich oils by the tablespoonful as well. (For those of you still traumatized by a childhood that involved daily doses of cod liver oil, rest assured that the ensuing decades have seen the flavour of fish oils improve dramatically.)

The foundation of great nutrition, says personal nutritionist Theresa Albert, is controlling your blood sugar levels, and this process starts with a nutritious breakfast that contains at least 10 grams of protein and 10 grams of fibre. (I remember hearing this advice before, from cardiologist and TV host Dr. Mehmet Oz, who advised eating 10 grams of protein within thirty minutes of waking. The problem is that I mistakenly thought he said 30 grams of protein within ten minutes of waking. The next morning I woke up and ran to the kitchen, where I grabbed a small container of yogourt. It contained 3 grams of protein. I thought I'd have to eat ten of them each morning just to make my protein count. I went online and double checked his advice, and soon realized my mistake.) Albert recommends a "magic muesli" containing Greek yogourt and a mix of hemp seeds, chia seeds, fruits and nuts.

Fibre is often relatively deficient in our diets. In his fascinating talk "Sugar: The Bitter Truth," Dr. Robert Lustig points out that fifty thousand years ago, our ancestors consumed between 100 and 300 grams of fibre each day. Today we consume on average 12 grams. Nutritionists used to think that the primary function of fibre was to fill the gut and turn off ghrelin, also known as the "hunger hormone." But Albert says researchers now understand that as fibre is digested, it passes into the bloodstream and then triggers in the brain the production of leptin, the "satiety hormone," which signals that the body is full.

Controlling blood sugar comes down to eating protein- and fibre-rich meals, and eating on a regular basis. "Most people wait far too long to eat," says Albert. When they do, they experience a hunger crash, or a drop in blood sugar levels. The result is often a last-minute grab for a nutrient-low and calorie- and sugar-rich snack, like a pastry or a sugary granola bar. This causes blood sugar levels to spike, which then triggers a release of cortisol, the stress hormone. Cortisol not only suppresses the immune system, but also shortens the telomeres—little caps on the edge of our chromosomes that serve a range of functions, including promoting longevity. By controlling blood sugar levels and also eating lots of DHA, we can maintain the health of our telomeres, a crucial step in healthy aging.

It goes without saying that one of the best ways to control blood sugar is to reduce overall sugar intake. As much as I adore sugar, I know that when it comes to our health, it really is the devil. According to Dr. Lustig, a pediatric endochrinologist at the University of California, San Francisco, who specializes in treating obese children, the average American woman consumes 335 more calories per day than in 2004, mostly from sugary drinks. These sugary drinks, in turn, derive their sweetness from high-fructose corn syrup. This particular type of sugar raises small LDL fat counts—which can lead to heart disease—but also suppresses leptin production, which essentially turns off the feeling of fullness. The more sugar we eat, the less able we are to feel full. And high sugar consumption can also lead to increased risk for Type 2 diabetes.

In 2014, this range of risks associated with high sugar intake prompted the World Health Organization to urge people to lower their sugar intake to less than 5 percent of daily calories. In fact, Dr. Francesco Branco, the head of nutrition for the World Health Organization, called sugar "the new tobacco." For some of us, lowering sugar consumption to less than 5 percent of total caloric intake could mean major lifestyle changes that go beyond avoiding chocolate bars. Many of our staples, such as breads and cereals, contain sugar, as does wine. Theresa Albert points out that drinking two glasses of red wine could put you at the upper limits of sugar consumption for the entire day. One easy way to cut out sugar is to avoid sugary drinks altogether. (I'll get to alcohol in a moment.)

Theresa Albert also recommends that older women take a

daily magnesium supplement. She says that nutrient-depleted soils caused by commercial farming practices now mean that up to two-thirds of Canadians are magnesium deficient. Magnesium contributes to improvement in a number of body functions, including nerve-impulse conduction, muscle contraction and heart rhythm. I have used magnesium supplements for years to prevent leg cramps.

¶ A Note on Alcohol

I recently stopped at a liquor outlet to pick up a bottle of wine for a potluck and was astounded by the number of alcoholic drinks that were specifically marketed to women: SkinnyGirl Vodka, Cupcake wine and so on. As Ann Dowsett Johnston writes in *Drink: The Intimate Relationship between Women and Alcohol,* alcohol consumption by women is on the rise, and when it comes to problem drinking, "women are closing the gender gap." The U.S. Centers for Disease Control estimates that alcohol is the leading cause of preventable death after tobacco and the combination of poor diet and inactivity.

Alcohol has increasingly deleterious effects on a woman's body as she ages. Muscle mass is what helps us to metabolize alcohol, and as we age, we gradually lose muscle mass, thus diminishing our body's ability to properly filter alcohol. Alcohol intake is also a risk factor for certain illnesses such as breast cancer. The Centers for Disease Control estimates that 23,000 women die each year from alcohol-related harms, half of which are related to binge drinking.

So how much is too much? Canada's current safe drinking

guidelines suggest that women should not consume more than ten drinks per week, with no more than two drinks in a sitting. Experts say the guidelines for older women should be lower than this, due to our decreased capacity to metabolize alcohol.

Alcohol consumption can lead to all sorts of health problems—for one, there are the adverse reactions with drugs, especially as we enter an age where we will likely be prescribed more medications. Alcohol consumption also compromises our balance, which can lead to falls and disabilities. And it can damage the stomach lining, liver and heart, increase the chance of some cancers and lead to poor sleep.

I still have a small glass of Scotch on occasion; after all, a Scottish heart surgeon told me on my television show that he "would not underestimate the medicinal value of a wee dram of Scotch"! Nevertheless, I firmly believe that at a certain age, women should be mindful of their alcohol consumption.

I could probably write an entire chapter about the health benefits of cannabis. Suffice it to say that cannabis offers myriad health benefits, especially when it comes to reducing pain. When I was suffering from acute pain related to my shoulder injury, I was prescribed cannabis in a pill form, nabilone. This offered the pain relief, minus the high. I took two before I went to bed, and for the first time in months was able to get a proper sleep.

I still enjoy the occasional joint. Pot is to me as the occasional glass of wine is to many others. I like the way I suddenly notice the colours of my flowers, the way I see the moon with fresh eyes. My imagination becomes more vivid and active, and I feel happy. I remember a few years ago talking to some leading psychiatrists after a talk I did. One of them said, in all serious-ness, that the minute he entered a nursing home, he would make a plan with his kids to bring a bong to his window every evening at seven. He understood the pain-relieving and relaxational benefits of a little puff. While Aspirin is still, in my mind, the miracle drug (old school, but it works for me, to ease both headaches and joint pain), cannabis is a close second.

Lobby for Change

Taking charge of one's health is simple: exercise, eat a protein-and DHA-rich diet, get proper sleep, and avoid alcohol and other harmful substances such as tobacco. But experts in older women's health like Dr. Tannenbaum say that baby boomer women can have the biggest impact by working collectively to lobby for chan-ges to the health care system that would benefit their cohort.

For instance, because women often outlive their husbands and thus end up spending years of their older life alone, servi-ces that assist them to access fitness classes would contribute to their overall health. The government pays for sleeping pills and medication, but what about cognitive or group therapies to give women the tools to deal with the emotional challenges of aging (which almost always manifest themselves in the body)? "Empowered baby boom women have the capacity to change the way health service are delivered and how money is allocated to preserve health," says Dr. Tannenbaum. The time to lobby for a health system that truly supports older women isn't when we are ill or disabled. The time is now.

CHAPTER 7

KEEP THAT BRILLIANT MIND

Reduce your risk factors for neurodegenerative
disease and psychological disorders.

All my life I have struggled with bipolar disorder, a brain condition that causes extreme shifts in mood, energy and activity levels. Once known as manic-depressive disorder, bipolar disorder has deeply affected every aspect of my existence—my relationships, my career and my physical health. In fact, it was not until my late forties that I truly gained control of my mind, thanks to appropriate medication and psychotherapy.

The process of recovering from bipolar disorder and staying mentally healthy has inspired in me an enduring appreciation of the human brain. This magnificent organ consumes 60 percent of the body's total oxygen intake and is ultimately responsible for all that we do, say and are. The brain has an enormous capacity to think, govern, heal and restore. It is a natural marvel. Caring for and protecting the brain is perhaps one of the greatest gifts we can give ourselves. This is especially important in our fifties and sixties. As we get older, our vulnerability to psychological and neurological problems increases. Alzheimer's disease, dementia, cognitive impairment, depression, anxiety disorder—these are the major threats to our mental health. In fact, some brain experts suggest these—neurodegenerative disease in particular— are among the most significant health and social threats to our society as a whole over the next few decades.

And while dementia poses a threat to brain health, it is certainly not the only challenge. The trials and tribulations of aging, including loss, financial hardship, declining health and social isolation, can also put older women at risk of developing mood disorders such as depression. And throughout our lives, women are more likely than men to experience depression and anxiety. Depression risk peaks around menopause, but a woman's unique life circumstances can make her especially vulnerable to the disorder later in life.

Given our increased vulnerability to conditions such as dementia and depression, it is critically important that women educate ourselves about neurological and psychological disorders, and do everything we can to reduce our risk factors and prepare for what's ahead.

Why Be Concerned about Brain Health?
So why is it that women are especially vulnerable to the neurological and psychological conditions of older age? Physicians offer up a number of possible explanations, but never before providing

this one caveat: *we're not totally sure.* For all the advances made in the fields of psychiatry and neurology, many aspects of how and why the brain functions as it does are still a mystery. For example, while we know that one of the reasons women are more suscept- ible to dementia is that they live longer, scientists also know there are other factors at play—but they still don't know what those factors are.

Even without a complete picture, however, it's helpful to understand some of the underlying causes that make us uniquely vulnerable to cognitive and psychological disorders so that we can do our best to prevent them.

The first and most obvious risk factor is age. While neuro- degenerative diseases can affect people in their forties and fifties, they primarily target adults over 65, of whom there are more and more each year. Indeed, after the age of 65, your risk of develop- ing dementia doubles every five years.

Another major risk factor for neurological or psychological disorders is stress. "You cannot underestimate the influence of life stressors," says Dr. Tony Phillips, the founding director of the Insti- tute of Mental Health at the University of British Columbia. Dr. Phillips's own research has shown that stress hormones actually modify the circuits in the brain's frontal lobe—the part of the brain that allows us to think rationally and plan ahead. And while this stress-induced modification can happen at any stage of life, as we age the frontal lobes become even more vulnerable to stress.

In an unfortunate twist, it's common for older adults to experi- ence disproportionately more life stressors as they age, says Dr. Phillips. I need only look at my own life and at the lives of the older women I know to see that this is true. The older we get, the more frequently we face the loss of friends, family members and spouses. In my twenties, thirties and forties, it was rare to meet women of my age who faced serious health problems. Today, alas, among my older friends, diagnoses of chronic illness are much more common. Poverty too, which places enormous stress on people, disproportionately affects women. Another source of stress in the older woman is uncontrolled pain. As pain-causing illnesses such as arthritis increase, so does our likelihood of becoming depressed.

Low estrogen levels can also negatively impact the brain. While estrogen is most often thought of as a reproductive hormone, it is in fact a pivotal brain hormone for both men and women. In men, testosterone is actually converted to estrogen once it reaches the brain. Certain crucial aspects of cognition, especially accessing and processing memories, are facilitated by estrogen. So as estrogen levels plummet after menopause, women become more vulnerable to memory loss.

Social isolation is another profound risk factor for both neurodegenerative disease and psychological disorders such as depression. As we age and lose friends or partners, retire from work or become physically incapable of activities we once enjoyed, isolation increases—and in turn elevates the risk for mental and brain health problems.

There are a number of things we can do to reduce our risk factors for neurodegenerative disease as well as psychological disorders such as depression and anxiety. Before we explore these strategies, however, we take a closer look at the biggest threats to our brain health and mental wellness as we age.

Dementia

As I look forward to the next two decades, I picture a vibrant future filled with family, fun and purpose. But if there is one fear that lingers over this idyllic picture, it's the threat of dementia.

According to the Alzheimer Society of Canada, as of 2010, 35.6 million people worldwide were living with dementia—that's more than our nation's population. Meanwhile, the global prevalence of dementia is expected to double every twenty years, with 115.4 million people living with some form of dementia by 2050.

"It's truly frightening," says Dr. Sandra Black, a cognitive neurologist at the Sunnybrook Health Sciences Centre in Toronto. According to the Alzheimer Society of Canada, the total economic burden of dementia, which includes direct health costs, opportunity costs and lost income of unpaid caregivers, along with other indirect costs, was $15 billion in 2008. The annual economic burden is expected to reach $293 billion by 2040. Given the changing demographics, which have seen a disproportionate rise in the number of elderly compared to the number of working-age, taxpaying adults, the economic picture is particularly grim. "How will we as a society pay for that?" asks Dr. Black.

A 2014 survey from CARP, a national association that lobbies for the rights of older Canadians, revealed many of its members believe that, as a country, we are unprepared to deal with the economic impact of age-related illnesses.

As women, we are especially vulnerable. Dementia prevalence is higher for older women than for men. Alzheimer Society of Canada research suggests that 72 percent of the Canadians who are currently living with the disease are women. In addition, women shoulder the majority—some experts estimate as much as three-quarters—of the caregiving burden. This is not to suggest that men are not caring for parents or spouses who live with dementia—indeed, I personally know men who are doing so. The fact remains, however, that of the many millions of hours family members devote each year to largely unpaid dementia care, the vast majority are spent by women.

Research from the Alzheimer Society of Canada also indicates that three-quarters of all Canadians know someone with dementia. I certainly know someone with dementia—or perhaps better put, I used to know her.

Lyn is one of my oldest friends, one who stood by me through thick and thin. I met her when I was a new bride to Pierre, and we have remained close for over forty years. Our children are similar in age, and both of us have sons on Parliament Hill. As two political matriarchs, we found our friendship charged with a touch of friendly maternal competitiveness as we watched our sons advance in the Liberal Party. But that spirit of competitiveness was always laced with a sense of mutual enjoyment, cheerleading and support, and I felt lucky to have a friend who understood my life so well.

But then Lyn started behaving strangely. I first noticed it when she and I and some other friends were holidaying in Croatia. She'd chartered a luxurious catamaran, and we started each morning with a swim. As we prepared to jump off the deck and into the clear Adriatic, Lyn would shout, "Last one in is a rotten—" But then she'd stop, having forgotten what came next. This happened every morning. Eventually, someone else would chime in: "Rotten hippo!" "Rotten tomato!" Lyn's forgetfulness continued throughout the day, however. While the rest of us kept up an endless and varied commentary, she had five stories. Fabulous stories, delivered by a truly great storyteller—but still, only five. So every day at breakfast, lunch and dinner, we'd hear one of those five stories. Now and again I'd cast a sidelong glance at one of our other friends as Lyn launched into the third rendition of a tale. It was strange, we agreed, but once our trip was over and we all returned to our normal routines, I didn't give it further thought. So Lyn repeated herself, I thought. We all do that from time to time, don't we?

But we thought this only to comfort ourselves. It may be easy to mistake dementia for simple forgetfulness when you see someone occasionally. But when you spend a few days together in close quarters, the signs become unmissable.

Some time later I visited Lyn at her home in Ottawa and watched as she stood in front of her espresso machine and opened and closed the drawer beneath it for fifteen minutes. At first I thought she had lost something, but as her anxiety grew, I realized that my dear, intelligent friend had completely forgotten how to make espresso. I bustled in to help her and we were soon sitting down to coffee, but she was badly shaken and so was I. No longer could I minimize her absent-mindedness. What happened that afternoon made it all too clear that something profound was happening with her brain. I'm not sure what bothered Lyn more that day—the fact that she had become confused or that I had borne witness. She was a proud, independent woman, and I suspect she may have been hiding what was happening to her for some time.

Shortly afterwards she was diagnosed with Alzheimer's. Her

driver's licence was revoked and she became totally reliant on her husband to drive her to doctors' appointments and do simple chores like buying groceries or going to the bank. Then fate struck at him too—soon after her diagnosis, he suffered a severe cardiac problem that required surgery and a long recovery. Without his around-the-clock support, Lyn was completely vulnerable. She was forced to leave the family house for a nursing home.

I visit her often. She was one of the best-read people I'd ever met, and we once spent many an afternoon discussing literature. She doesn't read anymore, but she still enjoys having books around. Each time I visit I take her a wonderful new novel I've discovered, as a testament to our long-standing friendship.

Alzheimer's disease? Nursing homes? They were for *old* people, not for me and my friends! I was devastated. I have experienced tremendous loss in my life, but nothing like this. When I visited and took her to lunch in a nearby restaurant, Lyn was present in body but not always in mind. There were times when I stared at her over the table, listening as she urged me to take immediate action on some event that had happened years ago, and I mourned the wise, witty friend I had lost. Invariably a niggling question whispered through my mind: Could I be next?

I hate to think this way, but I must be a realist. The Alzheimer Society of Canada projects that by 2031, 1.4 million Canadians will be affected by dementia. While dementia is by no means a normal part of aging, it is certainly a threat we must prepare for. And that begins with understanding what exactly we are up against.

Dementia refers to a family of neurodegenerative diseases that affect memory, judgment, reasoning and a person's mood and behaviour. The disorders are caused by a buildup of proteins in the brain that, over time, kill healthy brain cells. In general, different types of protein correspond to different types of dementia. We now know that these changes in the brain can begin up to thirty years before a person shows any outward signs of trouble. Scientists say that a person has dementia when these brain changes affect their ability to function normally.

There are several different types of dementia. Alzheimer's disease is by far the most common, accounting for roughly two-thirds of all dementia cases in Canada. Vascular dementia is the next most common form, making up another one-fifth. The other main forms of dementia include Lewy body dementia, frontotemporal dementia, Creutzfeldt-Jakob disease, Parkinson's disease and Huntington's disease.

Vascular dementia is caused by problems in the supply of blood to the brain. If the system of blood vessels within the brain becomes damaged, blood can no longer reach the brain cells and they die. Vascular dementia is triggered by a number of conditions. Stroke-related dementia is the result of a stroke cutting off the blood supply to the brain. Small-vessel disease—a condition more common in women than in men—happens when the small blood vessels deep within the brain become damaged. Although vascular dementia is the second most prevalent type of dementia, the good news is that in many cases it can be halted by lifestyle changes. Eat a heart-healthy diet, quit smoking, drink less alcohol and get lots of exercise—these are ways to reduce the underlying causes of vascular dementia, including high blood pressure, high cholesterol and diabetes.

Alzheimer's disease is caused by plaques and tangles that accumulate throughout the brain over time. The plaques are the buildup of beta amyloid proteins. The tangles are the "skeletons" that these proteins leave when the neurons degenerate. The disease progresses through various stages but is ultimately fatal because it destroys brain cells. The person living with the disease "forgets" how to perform the activities necessary for survival, such as eating, moving and communicating.

While most people link Alzheimer's and other forms of dementia with memory loss, forgetfulness is just one of many symptoms, says Dr. Carmela Tartaglia of the Tanz Centre for Research in Neurodegenerative Diseases at the University of Toronto. "Your brain has changed and you're no longer able to do the things you did before," she says. Decreases in the ability to organize and plan, communicate, recognize and relate to people, navigate through space and conform to social norms are all potential signs of Alzheimer's and other forms of dementia, as are changes in behaviour or mood. If you are experiencing consistent challenges in these areas, talk to your doctor. The problem, of course, is that diagnosing Alzheimer's or any other form of dementia can be challenging.

"Unfortunately, in neurodegenerative diseases, we don't have good markers," says Dr. Tartaglia. "When you want to test for diabetes, you go to your doctor, you get a blood test and they tell you, 'You're diabetic.' But dementia is not like that."

To diagnose dementia, physicians currently home in on a pattern of behaviour or symptoms rather than a single predictive test. The first step is gathering a patient's story—understanding the symptoms she has been experiencing, and the severity and duration of those symptoms. The next step is to perform cognitive function tests that explore language, memory, and special and executive reasoning within the brain. If the patient's score is out of line with what is normally expected of someone her age, the doctor will schedule an MRI to further examine the brain.

We still lack effective markers for most forms of dementia, but recent years have seen scientific breakthroughs. In early 2014, researchers from the University of Rochester Medical Center published the results of a study in *Nature Medicine* that showed a new blood test was accurate in predicting Alzheimer's 90 percent of the time. They were quick to point out that the bio-markers they developed are currently for use in clinical research only, but they certainly mark a step forward not only in our understanding of the disease, but also in our future ability to screen for the illness.

The notion of Alzheimer's screening brings up a compelling question, though—what use is it to have early diagnosis of a disease we can't cure? What's more, such a test may raise false fears. It's possible, and scientifically documented, for a person to have Alzheimer's or other neurocognitive diseases but not show signs of dementia. In one study that used positron emission tomography (PET) brain imaging to take images of the brains of live patients, just over a fifth that showed physical signs of dementia (e.g., protein buildup) had no outward signs of cognitive impairment.

How is this possible? Dr. Black calls it one of the many "mysteries" of dementia, but points to tantalizing clues in the study of a group of Minnesota nuns that is still regarded as a landmark investigation into why some people suffer dementia while others don't—even when both groups show evidence of a buildup of plaques and tangles. Begun in the mid-1980s by epidemiologist Dr. David A. Snowden at the University of Minnesota and later moved to the University of Kentucky, the Nun Study followed about 680 nuns ranging in age from 75 to 103 at the Convent of the School Sisters of Notre Dame in Mankato, Minnesota. The nuns agreed to participate in annual tests of cognitive function— assessments that included how many words they could remember shortly after reading them on flashcards, how many animals they could name in a minute and whether they could accurately count coins. The nuns took part in physical exams and blood tests for nutrition. And crucially, they all agreed to donate their brains for further study after they died.

"The nuns were perfect for such a study," says Dr. Black. They lived consistent lives: they ate nutritious foods, usually from the same cafeteria; as teachers they were well educated; they exercised regularly; and because of the nature of their lifestyle, they rarely drank alcohol and didn't smoke. And the nuns lived a long time—much longer than their sisters outside the convent. Perhaps most important for the study, the convent kept excellent personal records that offered a detailed look at the lives of these women decades before some would ultimately show signs of cognitive impairment.

When researchers cross-referenced essays and personal biographies written by the nuns at the time they entered the convent, often in their late teens and twenties, they made a startling correlation between a nun's language skills early in life and the likelihood that she would develop Alzheimer's later in life. The nuns with more sophisticated language skills—defined by researchers as the number of ideas for every ten written words—were far less likely to develop Alzheimer's five or six decades later.

Pam Belluck's 2001 *New York Times* article on the study compared the early autobiographies and late-life cognitive and physical abilities of two nuns. Sister Nicoletta, then aged 93, crocheted, knitted, played "rousing card games" and walked several kilometres per day without a cane or walker. Her entrance essay included lines such as this: "After I finished the eighth grade in 1921, I desired to become an aspirant at Mankato but I myself did not have the courage to ask the permission of my parents so Sister Agreda did it in my stead and they readily gave their consent."

Compare this to the early essay of another nun, similar in age to Sister Nicoletta, who performed steadily worse in her cognitive tests and spent much of her time sitting quietly by a window: "After I left school, I worked in the post-office." Differences such as these were evident even among biological sisters who shared genes, upbringing and convent lives, but differed in terms of the "idea density" evident in their entrance essays. The underlying theory here: mental acuity protects the brain from Alzheimer's and dementia.

Depression and Other Mood Disorders

While dementia receives perhaps the lion's share of attention when it comes to matters of older adulthood and brain health, depression too poses a threat to mental wellness. Though there is a genetic component to most mood disorders, depression in particular is known as a "multi-factorial" illness—a disorder that stems from a number of different causes. Dr. Marie-France Rivard of the University of Ottawa points out that there is an "accumulation of these factors when people age." Loss, chronic pain, declining health, social isolation, poverty—all these factors become more common as we get older, and together they put us at increased risk of becoming depressed.

But there are other, lesser-known causes. For instance, Dr. Rivard points to new research linking sleep apnea—a common yet often undiagnosed condition in post-menopausal women—with increased rates of depression.

Memories of early life trauma or loss, such as the loss of a parent in childhood, can be triggered by a loss in later adulthood that, when combined with other challenges related to aging, launches a depressive episode. "It can be the straw that breaks the camel's back," says Dr. Rivard. Indeed, she says the straw and camel metaphor is a useful way to understand depression in older adults: "When you're younger and don't have other chronic medical conditions, when you have lots of other things going on around you in your life, you wouldn't be as vulnerable to depression. But in old age it's common to accumulate many risk factors for depression, so the illness appears."

The multi-factorial nature of depression, combined with the increased risk of developing several of these contributing factors in older age, means that in many cases people who have not experienced depressive episodes in their lives have their first taste of depression as older adults. And this, says Dr. Rivard, can present problems in diagnosing and treating the illness. For starters, many in this particular group wait too long to ask for help. If you or someone you know struggles with depression, know this: there is no shame in having a mental illness. The shame is in having one and doing nothing about it.

"They feel ashamed that they have depression. They tell me, 'My children are good and I have enough money,'" says Dr. Rivard. "They feel there's no logical explanation for why they feel so poorly, and so they wait to ask for help."

One of the challenges of diagnosing depression in older adults is that unlike in younger adults or youth, depression doesn't always correspond with depressed mood. For instance, chronic pain associated with arthritis is stressful and exhausting for the mind and body and can lead to depression. But as Dr. Rivard points out, if you were to ask a patient what was "wrong" with her, she'd be far more likely to bring up her aching hip joint than her depression. "They think, 'Of course I feel bad. I'm in such pain.'" In this way, a woman might treat the physical condition—pain—but miss out in treating the depression. And so it lingers, and causes even more problems, such as social isolation and a failure to eat properly.

For me, depression feels like a crushing weight. Dr. Rivard suggests a useful acronym for helping to identify symptoms of depression in older adults: SIGECAPS.

> S: A change in sleep patterns. In some cases, this could mean someone begins experiencing difficulty falling or staying asleep. In other cases, a person may suddenly feel like sleeping all day. Sleep apnea also falls in this category.

I: Interest. Specifically, the person loses interest in things that once gave a sense of purpose or pleasure.

G: Guilt. "We all make mistakes in life," says Dr. Rivard. "But what concerns us is when a person ruminates excessively on past mistakes."

E: Loss of energy. This symptom can be tricky to identify because of our attitudes about age, says Dr. Rivard. "The loss of energy that is due to depression is often attributed to aging," she says. The key is to compare your energy loss to your typical energy level. So if you used to easily mow your front lawn but suddenly lack the energy to do so, it's worth talking to your doctor.

C: Concentration and cognitive problems. When someone is suffering from depression, it's not uncommon for her to have difficulty concentrating and registering information—both of which might cause others to think she is having memory problems. And this could translate into a false diagnosis of early cognitive impairment. Dr. Rivard urges women who are experiencing cognition problems to ask to be checked out for depression.

A: Appetite and digestion. Loss of appetite is a common symptom of depression in older adults, as are digestive problems such as constipation. In fact, it's common for constipation to be the primary reason older adults consult their physicians, and this has prompted Dr. Rivard to train family doctors to do a quick screen for depression any time an older patient presents with digestive problems.

P: Psychomotor changes. These show up in two ways. Psychomotor agitation refers to the behaviour of a person who cannot sit still—she wrings her hands, paces the floor, is unable to sit or stand in one place for more than a few minutes. Psychomotor retardation refers to the opposite behaviour—a person's response time slows down dramatically. For instance, you might ask her a question and it will take her a long time to answer you. Both types of psychomotor changes are potential signs of depression.

S: Suicidal ideation—a preoccupation with death. It's common to think of suicide as a young person's tragedy, but the statistics on suicide among older adults is surprising. Suicide rates in elderly men are as high as those in men aged 20 to 25, for instance. And though suicide rates for older women peak between ages 55 and 65, Dr. Rivard points out that suicides may be under-reported. "They may die from not eating properly, or by taking to their beds and not doing anything anymore. It's hard to estimate the suicide rates for people who quietly end their life." While suicide attempts are much higher in younger women, completion rates are higher among older women. "If you look at the 20-year-old women population, the rates may be around twenty to thirty attempts for one completed suicide. If you look at the elderly population, the rates go down to three to four attempts for each completed suicide."

While neurodegenerative disease and depression are among the biggest threats to mental wellness in older women, there are other, lesser-known threats of which Dr. Rivard says women should be aware. First and foremost is the changing impact of certain prescription and over-the-counter medications on the female brain.

Women who experience anxiety disorder may be placed on tranquilizers or benzodiazepine, such as Ativan. Such treatments may be appropriate for younger women, but older women should avoid them, says Dr. Rivard. These drugs affect not only memory but also balance, thus putting women at increased risk of head trauma (which can increase the risk of developing dementia). For those tempted to take tranquilizers to help them sleep, Dr. Rivard instead recommends non-pharmacological interventions—getting plenty of exercise during the day, practicing relaxation techniques, avoiding alcohol and ensuring you have a good mattress. In cases where women absolutely do need sedation, Dr. Rivard suggests that doctors prescribe mild antidepressants, which have a sedative effect but low anticholinergic properties—in other words, they don't affect the neurotransmitters in the brain responsible for alertness and memory.

Strategies for Nurturing the Brain
Over the last decade, I have delivered hundreds of talks across North America about brain health and mental wellness. A cen-

tral component of my message is that recovering from a mental illness and remaining mentally healthy is a process that begins when you decide you want to become well, and then you find the right experts to assist you. The process does not happen overnight. Rather, it's a series of baby steps.

When I emerged from the worst of my mental breakdown, I was weak and malnourished. I decided to invest in workouts with a personal trainer. Alan was young, handsome and kind, and I went to his gym twice a week. It was expensive—there were no new shoes to be had when I was working out with Alan—but I loved feeling my body grow healthier and stronger.

I was fortunate to have people in my life like lovely Ally, who understood that recovery happens gradually. She helped me celebrate each one: "Mom! You're going out on a lunch date? Good for you!" Recovery is a process you cannot tackle alone.

One of the things I've learned from this work—as well as my own experience with bipolar disorder—is how fearful we are as a society when it comes to mental health. In fact, the term *mental health* has become synonymous not with health, but with illness. A great deal of stigma and fear surrounds almost any issue related to brain health. And the trouble with fear is that we often run away from it. I have seen this at the individual level—people put off talking to their doctors about their symptoms because they are afraid of being diagnosed with a psychological or neurodegenerative disorder. And I also see it at the national level. Despite reams of evidence that show an alarming increase in the prevalence and economic burden of dementia, in Canada we still do not have a national strategy to cope with these diseases. Individual and collective inaction is shameful. Psychological disorders are treatable and not a function of old age. Though neurodegenerative illness is, for the most part, incurable, some treatments have been shown to slow its progression. And whether we are talking about depression or Alzheimer's, there is plenty we can do to optimize brain health and mental wellness.

The recipe for maintaining a healthy brain isn't much different from the one we follow to stay physically healthy—proper nutrition, restorative sleep and plenty of exercise. We explored these in detail in Chapter 6, but there are a few things worth noting about brain health and lifestyle.

When it comes to maintaining a healthy brain, it's important to consume plenty of essential fatty acids, which are found in fish oils, olives and other foods in the so-called Mediterranean diet. Exercise—especially vigorous exercise—is generally the first prescription for neurodegenerative disease, as it supplies the brain with much-needed oxygen. For this reason, getting lots of exercise can slow down the progression or appearance of dementia. In addition, exercise promotes social engagement and interaction, which offers protection against both dementia and depression.

The positive effect of brain stimulation can't be overstated, says Dr. Tony Phillips. "The brain seeks challenging problems . . . an active and engaged brain is self-repairing." In fact, researchers suggest that the reason education and stimulation protect the brain is that they stimulate the development of new neural pathways that actually create brain "reserves."

This doesn't mean we all have to run out and start madly doing sudoku. Rather, the emphasis should be on taking part in activities that interest and delight you, preferably in the company of others. Auditing a university or college course, attending lectures, learning a new language, going out to the movies or other performances, walking through a new section of town, making something for dinner you've never cooked before—all these things stimulate the brain. I have a girlfriend in her eighties who has learned to play chess, primarily because she had a lifelong interest in the game, but also because it gives her an opportunity to meet new people and stimulate her brain. Now 87, Martine takes care to dress beautifully each day, and heads out for wonderful long bike rides on the weekends. I admire her immensely.

Another effective strategy is to focus on right thinking. I define "right thinking" as that which results from a close examination of my thoughts to ensure they make sense. Reading a good self-help book (such as one on cognitive behavioural therapy) can help straighten out your thinking. But nothing beats a conversation with a therapist. Therapy can give us the space and guidance to unwind our tightly bound thoughts, shake them off, examine them and let them go.

Just as important as the things we can do as individuals to preserve brain health are the things we can do as a collective. The sad truth is that Canada is unprepared to cope with the fast-growing number of people living with dementia. A 2014 CARP poll of more than 2,300 members across Canada revealed that 81 percent believe not enough is being done. "I can't overemphasize the need to have an effective strategy around dementia," says Dr. Phillips. "Imagine having a health system where half of our society is looking after the other half."

So what should be included in a dementia strategy? Most experts agree that caregiver support—including work leave, training and other resources such as temporary paid relief care—is at the top of the list. Statistics from the Alzheimer Society of Canada show the staggering burden of caring for family members with dementia. In 2011, family caregivers—a quarter of whom are seniors themselves—spent more than 444 million unpaid hours looking after someone with dementia or another form of cognitive impairment. This unpaid time represented $11 billion in lost income and 227,760 full-time equivalent employees in the workforce. By 2040, it is estimated that family caregivers will devote 1.2 billion unpaid hours per year to caring for relatives with cognitive impairment, including dementia. And if the economic toll is astounding, the personal toll can be tragic. Up to 75 percent of family caregivers will develop psychological illness and roughly a third will experience depression. CARP is lobbying for other supports to alleviate the caregiver burden including training for health care providers, more home care resources and better dementia care within the formal health care system.

We also need to invest more in dementia and Alzheimer's research. The Weston family donated $50 million in 2014 to a new centre that will research neurodegenerative disease in an effort to better understand, diagnose and ultimately treat these illnesses. This is a promising start, but more research money is required.

Another much-needed support is exercise programs for people with dementia. As I mentioned earlier, exercise is often the main prescription for people who have been diagnosed with dementia or cognitive impairment. The problem is that as the illness progresses, exercising socially becomes more challenging. Dr. Carmela Tartaglia runs weekly exercise classes for dementia sufferers. "This is not your average workout at GoodLife," she says. From finding a suitable location to ensuring participants have transportation to the class, Dr. Tartaglia says making each class happen is an heroic feat. But the results speak for themselves. "The caregivers say they notice a big difference" in the overall health of their charges. As a nation, we need programs like this in all our communities. But as Dr. Tartaglia points out, many communities across this country—especially smaller towns—are completely lacking in services for people living with dementia.

I strongly believe that we as baby boomers must lend our voices to the call for a national dementia strategy. While other jurisdictions such as the U.K. have had a national strategy in place for years, Canada lacks one, and currently the federal government has no plan to create one. Meanwhile, one in three of us will one day be living with some form of dementia. The statistics are both alarming and depressing. We must take action.

Another step we must take as individuals is to face our fears. Experts point out that it's not uncommon for people to delay seeking a diagnosis—either because they are afraid to learn the truth about their condition, or because they feel it is futile to be diagnosed with an incurable illness. Dr. Tartaglia disagrees. "When people don't have a diagnosis, it can create lots of animosity and tensions within a family." Because dementia can cause significant personality changes—your once sweet-tempered mother becomes rude or uncaring—it isn't uncommon for family members to grow distant initially. "They don't understand what's wrong, or why this person they love so much is being mean," says Dr. Tartaglia. Furthermore, because dementia affects judgment, sufferers can become vulnerable to fraud or theft, particularly if no one knows they are suffering. They might drain their savings accounts and spend unwisely. Dr. Tartaglia witnesses such horror stories frequently.

It's tempting to look at the burden of neurodegenerative illness and feel both frightened and helpless. But there is hope. By maintaining a healthy lifestyle, pursuing our interests, nurturing our social connections and lobbying for change, we can face this challenge together—and perhaps even rewrite the future.

CHAPTER 8

WATCH YOUR MONEY, HONEY

Plan well, to avoid outliving your retirement savings.

You cannot speak of a happy, vibrant and fulfilling life without considering money. Yes, the best things in life are free—love, relationships, nature—but money, for better or worse, makes the world go round. We use money for practically everything—to buy food, shelter, comfort and the freedom of choice.

Today, financial considerations set the parameters of my life: how much I work, the amount of vacation I take each year, where I live, how often I travel and what I wear. It's not that I love money—as much as I adore fine things, I have never been a materialistic person. It's one of the things that surprised Pierre most about me, as we negotiated our split. I didn't want his money. All I wanted was my freedom. "Money means nothing to me," I told him, and I meant it. But as a free, independent woman with a far smaller nest egg than I would wish for, I am acutely aware of my financial situation and how deeply it underscores my current reality and future choices. It was not always this way.

As was common in many households of my day, money was not a subject we discussed when I was growing up. It's curious to me that despite the importance of money in our lives it is still considered a taboo dinner table subject in so many families. But even though we didn't discuss money in the Sinclair family, I was deeply aware of the guiding principles my parents held with respect to cash. If you will forgive a mass generalization, my father was Scottish, and like many of his countrymen, he loved to save. Credit cards were not part of our family vernacular back then. If the money wasn't in the bank to buy something, we simply didn't buy it.

Despite his frugal ways, my father was generous where it counted. My mother had a healthy allowance for running the household. In fact, she considered it a salary. She budgeted well and shrewdly invested what was left over in stocks. Her financial savvy paid off: when my father retired *she* actually had more money than he, and spent the last part of her life as a wealthy elderly lady. As for me and my sisters, we were raised in comfort and all received a good education. When our schooling was done, our father helped us all get started in life, as we settled into our apartments and careers, at which point we were supposed to take over responsibility for our finances.

My first career was that of a prime minister's wife, and the lifestyle, which involved a tremendous amount of duty, simultaneously relieved me of some of the responsibilities that would have laid the foundation for the rest of my life. I'm talking about the earning and managing of money. I wore haute couture and ate off gold-rimmed plates that I did not pay for. I was surrounded by luxury, but I did not learn about financial responsibility. Pierre had inherited the bulk of his wealth, and therefore saw himself as a steward of money. His money did not belong to him, but to his descendants. This belief, combined with his disciplined and exacting nature, made him a frugal man, though without the generosity of my father. I was made to record every penny I spent and had no discretionary money of my own to manage—again, privilege without accountability.

When I left my marriage to Pierre at age 27, I was determined I would make it on my own. In one of the silliest moves of my life, I did not ask for any of the money that, as a prime minister's wife and the mother of his three children, I was surely owed. Over the next three decades, I worked at a number of different jobs—as a TV host, an author and a professional speaker. Like many women, I put my career on hold several times for the sake of raising my children. Because of this, I never really reached my own peak earning potential until I hit my fifties. And so today I stand before you as a woman who has at times led a life of relative privilege, a woman with children who can offer her a safety net should she need it, but also a woman who, like millions of other Canadians, does not have enough savings to retire.

My coming of age with respect to money really didn't happen until later in life. So when it comes to finances, I often feel like a scared teenager who has just learned to drive. There are many white-knuckled moments. At an age when many of my friends have retired, I am still working. A friend who is in a similar financial situation once described it in this way: "I eat what I kill." In other words, she had to work to have enough money to live. She had no one to support her, nor did she have enough savings to live on without working. Not a pleasant image, and yet a true one. Indeed, my freedom and independence—two things I prize—have always been linked to my ability to make money.

I always respected my mother for her insistence that she be paid for her work as a homemaker. How I have laughed after overhearing various men brag that their wives "haven't worked a day in their lives." Financial independence gives us power, and freedom. Yet I still have fears over money.

"Margaret," a dear friend once remarked, "you are always worrying about money, but you've always had it." This is true, of course—though over the years the money I had fluctuated dramatically. I remember, after Pierre and I divorced, complaining bitterly after robbers broke into my Ottawa home and stole a beautiful fur coat I'd been given during a trip to Japan. "Well, Margaret," he said, in all earnestness. "You no longer have a magnificent life. Why do you need such a magnificent coat?" Only a man would say that.

Now my life is much simpler.

The struggle to be solvent and free affects many women, particularly those living in developing countries and those north of 50. When it comes to money and power, men still have it all. Education is an important antidote. In parts of Africa, where I work, ensuring girls can go to school is essential to their financial future and that of their families, now and after they marry. But for women like me, too, education around finances is crucial. In researching this book, I sought the advice of experts in an effort to cure my fears once and for all.

I am lucky that I have a family safety net, but 2008 data from Statistics Canada reveals that many do not have any such support. At 8.6 percent, the poverty rate for older women is nearly double that of older men. Nearly one in five (18 percent) single women—be they unmarried, widowed or divorced—live in poverty. Older women on their own are thirteen times more likely to be poor than those living with families. The most distressing part of this data is that the research was conducted pre-recession, when overall poverty rates were their lowest in three decades. And even among those women who, like me, are living comfortably now, many worry that they are financially unprepared for the years ahead.

A 2014 poll conducted by Ipsos Reid for Sun Life Financial surveyed more than three thousand Canadians. Of those, just 28 percent said they expected to be able to retire by age 66, compared to 51 percent who felt they'd be ready when polled in 2008. More than a quarter (27 percent) of those surveyed in 2014 said they'd continue to work full time. Some of those who planned to work past the standard retirement age will do so because they love their work, but the majority—66 percent—cannot afford to retire. In fact, 20 percent of the respondents said they'd need to keep working to cover basic living expenses.

Another source—this time a 2012 report on Canadian retirement readiness from the consultancy McKinsey & Company—found that 41 percent of Canadians between the ages of 55 and 64 are not on track to retire. According to the report, a number of underlying structural forces have put pressure on the country's retirement system. First, our rapidly aging population has seen the 65-plus cohort increase from 11 percent of the total population in 1990 to a forecast 22 percent in 2030. Second, the stock market has shown limited returns since its turn-of-the-century peak, and has experienced major volatility since that time, which has hurt returns on individual and workplace retirement plans. And third, life expectancy and the average age of people entering the workforce has increased while the average retirement age has decreased. The result: the ratio of years in retirement to working years rose from 36 percent in 1980 to 53 percent in 2012.

If the financial realities are challenging for Canadians as a whole, they can be especially devastating for older women. Understanding the factors behind the financial challenges of older women is critical to addressing the problem—not only for us, but also for our daughters.

Economic Issues Faced by Older Women

Women face a host of economic challenges that overall make us less financially secure than men in older age. To begin with, we live longer than men. In the past, retirement plans were calculated to last twenty-five to thirty years past retirement. But for today's older woman, that just doesn't cut it anymore, says Caroline Dabu, vice-president and head of wealth planning at Bank of Montreal. "Now we've got a generation of women who could very well live to be 100." So a woman's retirement savings must last her up to that age.

As a certified financial planner, Dabu has spoken to thousands of people about their retirement over the years. And when she discusses with clients the prospect of living to 100, "most don't even want to think about it." There are two interrelated fears at play, says Dabu. The first is that they'll outlive their money (a distinct possibility). The second is that their health will fail and they won't be able to afford the health care they want, such as assisted living.

A second major economic challenge for women, says Dabu, is that "by and large, they have not put away or saved as much as men." And not only have they saved less, but they are likely to receive less from pension plans. According to CARP, in 2003, almost 70 percent of men over age 65 received income from a pension plan, while only 53 percent of women in the same age group had a plan. Women also receive, on average, lower Canada Pension Plan benefits. In 2009, the average monthly payout was $391.29 for women and $564.23 for men.

Why do we save less and receive lower pensions? According to CARP vice-president Susan Eng, women are suffering from still-entrenched sexism and social norms that reinforce a cycle of financial inequality. "You have to look at whether women have had equal opportunity to earn the kind of money that men did in order to prepare for their own retirement," she says. And the short answer to that question is a resounding no.

CARP data shows that currently, Canadian women working full time are earning 71 percent the income that men are earning across jobs. Women are more likely to find themselves in low-paying, part-time or informal work. And while this is changing, older women are also likely to have lower education levels than

their male counterparts, which also affects their career-long earning potential. Women of my generation in particular are far more
likely to have either halted or interrupted their careers in order to
raise children, which in turn affects their earning (and therefore
saving) potential and their contributions to either public or private pension plans. And today, while few of us are caring for our
children anymore (not full time, anyway), the majority of unpaid
caregivers for the elderly are women.

The final economic hurdle faced by women is singledom.
Living alone is costly. "Most women will find themselves spending their retirement years alone," says Dabu. Living alone in older
adulthood happens sometimes by choice and sometimes by cir-
cumstance, says Dabu. Bank of Montreal research indicates that
the average age of widowhood for women is 56 years old. What's
more, the highest rate of divorce for women occurs after age 56.
Known as "grey divorce," a marriage breakup in older age can
be devastating for women financially. On average, says Dabu, a
woman's standard of living drops by 45 percent after a divorce.
And when this happens to a woman in her sixties, "she's not in her
prime earning years anymore to make that up." For older women
who have worked primarily as family caregivers, grey divorce can
be especially difficult. Many have no choice but to try to re-enter
the workforce at a time when there are fewer job opportunities
for older adults.

I have experienced the painful drop in living standards that
comes after a divorce—twice. In my case, the dramatic change
in circumstances happened swiftly. One day I was living at the
prime minister's residence, the next I was not. Some women

experience this shift more gradually. Both scenarios are challenging and potentially devastating.

Reversal of Fortune

In the heyday of their marriage, Marney Simmons's ex-husband used to joke that financially they were "in the top 1 percent." Now she says, matter-of-factly and with a note of humour, that she is "at the bottom of the 99 percent."

They had married young and spent the early part of their marriage in Toronto, where they both worked to establish their careers. Within a few years, Marney's husband was offered a plum job in Tokyo. Marney was fascinated by foreign cultures, and happily quit her job to follow her husband there. Because she was unable to work in Japan, the couple decided it would be a great time to start a family. Marney gave birth to two boys during their stay in Japan, and then the couple moved to England in time for the boys to start school. They lived in England for most of the 1980s, and while her husband took on increasingly senior roles, Marney stayed home, running the household and supporting the children. By the late 1980s, the couple's relationship had become strained. They returned to Canada in 1990 and divorced three years later. Marney received a healthy settlement. She purchased a home in Ontario. She thought of going back to work, but as a newly single mother with two busy children, she couldn't find a job with enough flexibility that would allow her the time to drive her sons to after-school activities, cook nutritious meals and all the other caregiving activities she considered important. And so she stayed home and used her settlement money to raise her sons.

When her youngest son was in high school, she got serious about looking for a job. By then she felt her training was dated, and so she went back to university, eventually earning a master's degree in urban and regional planning from Queen's University. While she was studying, the dot-com bubble hit and wiped out $100,000 of her savings in one week. She was devastated by the loss, but reasoned that her education would stand her in good stead when it came to finding a new job. Equipped with her degree, she decided to honour a dream she'd had for years—to move close to the ocean. In 2004, she sold her Ontario home and moved "lock, stock and barrel" to Mulgrave, a quaint seaside town in Nova Scotia. She secured an excellent job as a land use planner, and soon set about beautifying her lovely 154-year-old home. For a time, life seemed perfect: her children were grown and self-sufficient, she had the home of her dreams and she was building a meaningful career.

Three years later, the job she was working at came to an end. She calmly began sending out resumés. Though she was upset at losing a job she loved, she was comforted by the fact that she still had a small financial nest egg. When work didn't come, she didn't lose hope, but decided to put her skills to use for the community. She became the mayor of Mulgrave in 2008, a position she held for more than four years. She took on small contract positions during that time, but despite sending out hundreds of resumés, was unable to find a job.

She's had limited luck. In several instances, she has made it through several rounds of phone interviews only to be turned down after her in-person interview, and later told by the employer that they found another candidate who "better fit the criteria." Marney can't help but feel that her age—she is 61—works against her, especially in instances where, given her training and experience, she seems a shoo-in for the job. "They take one look at my face and realize I'm not 30," she says ruefully. "Everything changes after that."

Meanwhile, her financial situation has grown increasingly grave. "Over all these years of raising children and going back to school, the money has dwindled away." Beginning a few years ago, she began selling off assets—a small cottage she owned, for instance—because she needed the money. She took out a line of credit, which she has dipped into to cover her monthly expenses as she continues to look for work. She put her seaside home on the market three years ago, but it has not yet sold. It now needs serious work but she doesn't have the money to pay for the upgrades. And given that she lives in an economically depressed area, it's possible she may not recoup the money she has put into the place. Desperate to find a job, she began giving her resumé to local restaurants and shops. She was told her retail experience was "too dated." While she remains positive and resolute, Marney knows she needs to make money—not only enough money to live on, but enough money to retire on. Some days, she feels the odds are stacked heavily against her. "I have all kinds of credentials and life experiences and feel so wasted and underutilized," she says. "I've exhausted all my resources."

In Marney's story we see some of the classic reasons why women face more financial hardship in older adulthood than men: interrupted careers lead to lower lifetime earnings, which in turn mean less ability to save and ultimately a small or non-existent nest egg. Ageist hiring practices exacerbate the problem. And supposedly rock-solid assets, like a beautiful home, can then become a leaden anchor. And so a talented, worldly, well-educated woman like Marney becomes an emblem of what many older women face. "There are a lot of older women who are brilliant but broke," she says. "No investments, no savings, no salary, no pension—I wonder what will become of us all?"

Marney spent decades of her adult life in charge of the day-to-day household finances. Financial experts say this daily money management is often the financial realm of women. But when it comes to the big picture of financial planning and money management, women often lack the knowledge and control they need to secure a healthy and sustainable financial life in older adulthood.

Women and Financial Literacy

Numerous studies have shown that women tend to have, on average, lower levels of financial literacy than men. I have certainly experienced this phenomenon first-hand. Both my husbands were more financially literate than I was, and sensing their greater knowledge, I ceded most financial decisions to them. At the time, it seemed to be a clear division of labour—the finances were "their issue" just as grocery shopping was mine. I later regretted outsourcing so much financial responsibility to the men in my life. This very dynamic I experienced could be one of the factors behind poverty in older women; studies link low financial literacy levels with poor financial outcomes, debt problems and insufficient retirement planning. In response to the 2011 Federal Reserve study *Aging and Strategic Learning*, which looked at 750 U.S. households, only 16 percent of households reported that the woman is the most financially knowledgeable person in the home. A report from Prudential Financial, which surveyed 1,250 U.S. women about their experiences and behaviours around money in 2010–11, found that despite women having gained financial knowledge and control over the last decade, they still lack knowledge about basic financial products such as mutual funds, annuities and long-term care insurance.

One of the main reasons for women's relative lack of financial knowledge is societal norms around household division of labour, which have rendered men primarily responsible for financial matters. What's more, even younger women, who have made tremendous gains in educational attainment relative to men, exhibit this relative lack of financial literacy. Even though the traditional household division of labour has evolved—I take it on good authority, for instance, that men now do their share of laundry and vacuuming—millennial women, the daughters we raised to be independent and self-sufficient, are in fact the *least* likely of all age cohorts surveyed to have a financial plan. This underscores an interesting trend—that women's financial literacy improves dramatically later in life, and is often tied to the mortality of her spouse.

Sarah, now 65, was a teacher when she met her future husband, Peter. She made a healthy salary; he was a recent graduate and international development volunteer who earned a weekly stipend of ten dollars—a pittance, even in the 1970s. They married and a few years later, Sarah left her job and they travelled overseas so that Peter could complete his PhD and start his career as a university professor. For the next eighteen years, Sarah stayed at home to raise their three children and look after the home, while Peter worked. To live comfortably on a single salary, the couple budgeted carefully. Sarah managed the day-to-day finances—buying groceries, clothing for the kids and other household necessities—while Peter paid the bills and assumed sole responsibility for the couple's financial plan—investments, insurance, RESPs and so on. The division of labour was clear, and it worked for them. And then Peter was diagnosed with cancer. Five months later, at age 58, he died.

In the months leading up to his death, Peter did his best to ensure Sarah understood the ins and outs of the couple's finances. They met numerous times with their financial adviser. But Sarah retained little of those conversations. She had other things on her mind. She was watching her husband slowly die. Every day he lost something—his hair, the curve of his cheeks, his ability to stand, and eventually his coherence. What consumed her during those painful months was caring for him and ensuring his last weeks were as comfortable as they could be. She was not thinking about the power bill or his pension plan.

But after his death, even as she dealt with the crushing weight of her grief, she was forced to try to absorb a body of financial knowledge that had taken Peter his lifetime to amass. For more than a year, she felt overwhelmed by the responsibility of managing the finances on top of all the other tasks that had once been part of his domain: dealing with the car, mowing the lawn, plowing the snow. It took her months to understand where her various investments were held, and how much money she actually had. Today, four years after his death, she is finally in control of her finances. She feels proud of herself, but says she wishes she had started her learning curve earlier.

Sarah's situation isn't far from the norm for many women, especially of our generation. We gave up control of the finances to focus on the household. The business of managing a household and nurturing children is important, consuming work. Even the Federal Reserve report suggests "it is efficient for members of a household to specialize in particular tasks." So if you ceded some control of your financial future to someone you loved and trusted because it was efficient and made sense at the time, you cannot fault yourself for it after the fact. Life can only be lived forward. But the Federal Reserve report also revealed that poor economic outcomes associated with widowhood may be linked to a woman's failure to acquire financial literacy early enough. On a positive note, the report found that 80 percent of women had caught up with their husbands' level of financial literacy before "the expected onset of widowhood." What's more, by the time widowhood was imminent, women tended to kick their knowledge acquisition into overdrive, following the stock market more closely and enhancing their overall skills.

Though it is indeed good news that women become more financially literate later in life—especially as widowhood approaches—this offers cold comfort to Candace Bahr and Ginita Wall, co-founders of the Women's Institute for Financial Education (WIFE), a non-profit that offers unbiased financial training to women throughout the United States.

"The worst possible time to play catch-up and build financial knowledge is when you're in the middle of a crisis and your spouse is dying, has died or has just told you he wants a divorce," says Wall, a San Diego–based accountant. Indeed, while the Federal Reserve report showed an acceleration in women's acquisition of financial literacy as the age of widowhood approached, it said little about divorce. Divorce and swift or unexpected widowhood can sneak up on women, offering us little or no time to build up our financial management skills—a body of knowledge that cannot be assumed overnight.

Unfortunately, this worst-case scenario is something she has seen many thousands of times in the twenty-six years since she and Bahr founded WIFE. In fact, the reason Wall and Bahr founded WIFE in the first place was that in the late 1980s, Bahr, who was a wealth manager, had five women enter her office over the course of a few months upset because they'd been financially blindsided after widowhood or divorce and wanted to learn more about their finances. "I was their financial adviser," Bahr says. "And I realized that while I knew a lot about their finances, I really didn't know enough about their lives." She met with Wall for lunch one day and they discussed the situation—as an accountant, Wall had seen many women in the same situation. "We looked at each other and said, 'What can we do to help more women learn about this stuff?'" And so WIFE was formed.

"The crisis with your partner hits. You don't know enough about what's been going on. Maybe you've been handling the day-to-day finances, but you don't know anything about the investments, or where the records are kept. He's got all the information on the stocks and funds you own. Suddenly debt surfaces that you didn't know anything about." For women dealing with the grief of divorce or their spouse's death, this sudden revelation of their lack of financial knowledge can be "completely overwhelming," Wall says. Wall and Bahr point to studies showing that 70 percent of women move to a new financial adviser following a divorce or the death of their husband, which suggests a low level of trust in the advisers they were seeing while married. The bottom line: women often have no one they trust and know well to turn to at a time when they need financial counsel most.

To combat the problem, Wall and Bahr launched a weekend financial seminar for divorced or widowed women called Second Saturdays. Now held across the country, a typical Second Saturday workshop will have between thirty to fifty women who come to listen to Wall, Bahr or other WIFE trainers go through the legal, financial and psychological issues of divorce or widowhood. "Frequently women will tell us, 'I was clueless about my financial situation. I didn't even know where to find the information.'"

Unfortunately, this lack of financial literacy often corresponds to a lack of confidence, and financial experts suggest that confidence plays a role in effective retirement planning. Without adequate financial knowledge, women are more likely to feel they are ill-equipped to make financial decisions, and therefore give over control of their finances to someone else. And so the cycle of financial disempowerment continues.

Take Back Control of the Purse Strings

In situations where I have limited knowledge, my tendency is to defer to the experts. The business section of any newspaper is the part I am most likely to discard without perusing. So for some years, I thought my best option was to find the best financial experts I could and rely on their advice. I could not have been more wrong.

"The last thing you want to do is abdicate responsibility to anyone else," says Pattie Lovett-Reid, a former TD Bank executive who is now CTV's chief financial commentator. "Not everyone wants to manage their own investment portfolio. Not everyone gets jazzed up about insurance, but what I tell women is that no one's going to care more about them and their financial future than they do. And so they really need to be involved in it."

Following my second divorce and the years I spent recovering from my breakdown, I had limited money. My sons gave me a monthly stipend that covered my bills but nothing else. The modest wage I earned at the location services company I worked for in Ottawa allowed me to pay for some extras—tickets to the opera or to movies, the odd trip to a restaurant. But after I became a professional speaker and published *Changing My Mind*, which was a bestseller, I realized I was finally in a position to begin saving for my retirement. Someone gave me the name of a fancy accountant who worked out of some plush offices in a Montreal high-rise. I met with him and told him my story and shared my dreams for how I wanted to live in my senior years. I suppose I must have offered a vivid picture of my ideal future, because he seemed to buy into it totally. I had gone to him to be cured of my money delusion—*I have led a privileged life that I can no longer afford.* I suppose I wanted him to confirm that for me.

Instead, he seemed to support the delusion. Perhaps it was because of my name and the fact that I was once a prime minister's wife. Maybe it was because he served mostly a group of rarefied and privileged clients. Either way, he was not the straight-talking money manager I'd hoped he was, and needed. Six months later I was no further ahead financially, nor did I really feel he had my back. At that point, another layer of the onion peeled away and I realized that I truly was the mistress of my own financial ship. And I knew then that my responsibilities included articulating exactly the sort of money manager I needed.

So I began asking around. When I went to meet Syd the first time, I knew I had found the right man. He is a tough, pragmatic man who works out of an unassuming box-like office in a decidedly not-swanky part of town. I tell him my dreams and he pierces those balloons kindly but matter-of-factly with the harsh news of what I can actually afford to do and what I cannot. One small but inconvenient part of my mental illness is that I find it nearly impossible to open envelopes. I told him this, and he handed me over to an assistant, who works with me to ensure my envelopes are opened, my bills paid and my taxes up to date.

As much as I trust Syd, however, I am conscious of my desire—and perhaps even conditioning—to be pampered. A small part of me still thinks I would love to be cared for. But I know now, at 65, that I cannot rely on a Prince Charming. Money is a tricky thing. It is easy to fall into the trap of wanting more of it—and greed only ever leads a person down the wrong path.

Bertie was a friend of mine who had worked her entire life as a nurse, but had saved little. She adored luxuries and envisioned a life for herself that was plush with fine clothes, international travel and beautiful jewellery. She was vocal about her wishes, but, given that she was single and earned a decent but certainly not extravagant salary as a nurse, I wrote off her desires for riches as little more than daydreaming. Then she went on a long holiday to Florida. When she came back, she had a new boyfriend— in his eighties. They were soon married. He built her a palatial home, where she now lives a luxurious but isolated life. It is hard to respect a person who trades love for money.

I remind myself of this whenever I resent having to work as much as I do. I must rely on myself. I must cultivate my own rational thinking and discipline to stay on top of my finances, to look after myself. I have only really had a well-paying career for the last decade. I'm in my mid-sixties and I simply must keep working and saving money for as long as possible. Syd may advise me, I may trust him, but I cannot turn my financial future over to him or anyone else. I must hold the purse strings.

Nest Egg 101

The first step in financial management is to quit procrastinating, says Pattie Lovett-Reid. "The thing that will hurt your financial plan most, and cause you the most stress, is to do nothing." Perhaps you avoid thinking or talking about money at all. Or maybe you have a vague notion of how you'd like to live in retirement, but you lack specifics.

Either way, if you care about your financial future at all,

experts say you start by doing two things: committing to becoming more financially literate, and creating a formal financial plan. While the idea of becoming more financially literate seems overwhelming to many women, myself included, it doesn't have to be stressful, says Lovett-Reid. "Think of it as an evolution. You don't wake up January first and say, 'Today I'm going to take complete charge of my financial situation.'" Rather, she says, it's a gradual process of asking questions, exploring, prodding and understanding your financial position both now and in the future. Talking to friends and relatives, reading magazines and newspapers, and attending seminars (most banks put on free retirement planning seminars each year) are all great starting points.

At around the same time, begin looking for a certified financial planner to help you build a plan. Understand that the end game of any strategy is freedom, says Caroline Dabu of Bank of Montreal. "This is about making the last decades of your life not only meaningful but sustainable. It's about having as much choice as possible—being able to afford to look after yourself and do the things you want to do."

You might be a do-it-yourself sort of person, and indeed all the major banks offer free online financial planning tools and calculators, but both Dabu and Lovett-Reid underscore the value of working with a third party. "I'm a certified financial planner, I work in the market, I talk about the market all day long and I have a passion for financial planning . . . and I [still] have an adviser," says Lovett-Reid. "It is just so helpful to have a third party to bounce ideas off. Everything related to money is emotional—an adviser helps you take some of the emotion out of it."

You can find certified financial planners everywhere—at the major banks, and at investment and insurance companies. When choosing one, Lovett-Reid says, the most important thing is to feel that you can trust them, and that they have your best interests at heart. "You need to ensure this person values you as a client, will meet with you and speak to you on a level you understand."

There are two main types of financial planners: some are paid a fee to help you manage your money; others earn a commission off your investments or various financial products, such as insurance. Lovett-Reid suggests asking how your financial planner is compensated, and when he or she is recommending a financial tool, ask how you will know whether this product serves *your* best interest versus *theirs*. Another important consideration is this: is the organization large enough that if something goes wrong or the adviser messes up (i.e., if you have to sue them), there is financial support?

Your choice of financial adviser is not something to take lightly. The Prudential Financial study found that women who work with financial advisers are more likely to feel they're on track than those who go it alone. And this feeling is usually backed up by reality—the McKinsey study about retirement readiness found that households with a financial adviser displayed significantly more readiness than those without—especially among the older adult cohorts. Whether you create a financial plan yourself, or get help, the reality is you need one. "Only 30 percent of Canadians have a financial plan," Dabu says.

In working with you to create a financial plan, your adviser will first help you clarify how much money comes into your household each month (income), and how much goes out (expenses). Next, your adviser will help you identify unnecessary expenses, luxuries that may be trimmed and other ways to maximize the money you have in order to set more aside for the future. Then, your adviser will help you create a net worth statement by adding up all your assets—savings and investments, the value of your house or other properties—and then subtracting your liabilities—credit card debt, mortgage, loans or lines of credit.

Your net worth statement becomes the basis of your financial plan, says Lovett-Reid, because it helps you establish relevant financial goals. For instance, if you have a negative net worth—meaning you have more liabilities than assets—the first step is to pay down your liabilities. Credit card balances should be eliminated as soon as possible. By the time you enter your sixties, you should have eliminated your mortgage entirely, or at least have prioritized paying it off. Alternatively, if you have a healthy net worth—and some women do discover they are worth more than they think, points out Lovett-Reid—your goals might involve creating a target nest egg amount, figuring out how much you need to save each month and then choosing investments that will help you reach your goal. Getting a handle on your finances means understanding monthly cash flow within the household, creating a net worth statement and then setting short- and long-term financial targets. Dabu recommends saving as much as possible and dividing these savings among various types of assets, such as investments, while at the same time setting aside an emergency fund—a pool of cash you can draw from to cover unforeseen expenses.

A note about putting money away: "Women will sometimes see saving and investing as the same thing," Lovett-Reid says. She points out that simply saving money—while an excellent first step—will not offer you much security in the long term. "Saving is a way to park your money before you invest it. But you need your money to work as hard for you as you've been working for it." In other words, first save, and then invest. If you're new to investing on your own behalf, Lovett-Reid says, a good balanced mutual fund is a great way to start.

Another cornerstone of a sound financial plan is insurance, says Dabu. According to a 2013 survey of 3,200 Canadian households from LIMRA, an international research and consulting organization for financial industry professionals, many Canadian households are underinsured. Life insurance, disability, critical illness and long-term care insurance should all be looked at and discussed with your financial adviser. Of all these things, long-term care insurance is most crucial. According to the LIMRA survey, 79 percent of Canadians are concerned about the cost or accessibility of long-term care.

There are many smart ways to use insurance as an estate planning tool. For instance, when you buy a participating permanent life insurance policy, you can use it as collateral to secure a tax-free loan. And the best part is that the loan is repaid with the benefit when you die. (This is as close to free money as we may ever get, so I like it.)

Like most people, I don't wish to think about the day when I may require help dressing or feeding myself. But I must face it.

We all must. Unfortunately, when it comes to calculating the true costs of retirement, many of us are still in la-la land.

Get Real about Retirement Planning

If you were to base your post-retirement lifestyle expectations solely on TV commercials, you'd think that life after work is an endless series of days on the golf green, cookery classes in Italy, holistic retreats in Sedona and extravagant gifts for grandchildren. Given what we now know about the lack of financial preparedness among Canadians, this rosy view is not only unrealistic, but also potentially damaging.

"We have to get away from this image of retirement as women taking trips to parts unknown," says Susan Eng of CARP. If, through prudent planning or luck or both, you have enough money to see you through the rest of your life *and* travel to parts unknown, this is wonderful. But the fact is that most of us don't. To understand just how much travel or Hermès scarf buying we can do during retirement, we first must understand how much money we need to *retire on.* And this is where many women with the best of intentions go astray. When it comes to planning for retirement, what's needed is clarity and detail, says Caroline Dabu. "Most people underestimate what's required to save for retirement until they get there. They just don't think about it in as much [detail] as they should."

One common pitfall, she says, is costing out the first half of retirement. So they take their monthly living costs, add in the price of a fun vacation each year, multiply it by the number of years they expect to live beyond retirement and come up with the dollar amount they believe they need. The problem is that they fail to calculate the costs of the second half of retirement—older age, when significant health care costs are likely to set in. As Susan Eng points out, despite our public health care system, there are still many new drugs that are not covered. It's not uncommon for living expenses to double when one spouse moves into a long-term care facility while the other is healthy enough to live at home. Or perhaps you are in a position to remain at home, but only if you invest in some substantial upgrades to allow you to do so, such as installing ramps, extra-wide doorways and so on.

Another hidden cost is providing long-term care for our own aging parents, who may not have saved enough themselves. And then there's the matter of our children. The fantasy is that they turn 18 and become financially self-sufficient. The reality is much different. Calculating how much—if any—money you wish to set aside for them, either as a legacy or as ongoing financial support, is another consideration.

Stay on top of your financial situation with what Ginita Wall and Candace Bahr call an annual "contingency day." If you are single—as many women are—do this activity on your own, or involve your children if you wish. If you're married, do it with your spouse. Contingency day is the day you review your financial plan and take stock of your assets. If you're behind on paying off debt, now is the time to focus on paying it down. If you have investments, make sure you know exactly what your assets are and where to find the supporting documentation. Figure out if any of your assets should be sold—the RV you never use, or the cottage you no longer have the energy to maintain. Review your will and estate plan to ensure they are current.

And don't underestimate the importance of making sure that the beneficiaries are up to date on all your investments, says Dabu. She has seen situations in which, because of a person's failure to update beneficiary information, money in major investment portfolios has gone to first wives rather than second wives even when the first marriage dissolved decades earlier.

When You Don't Have Enough Money to Retire On

So what happens if, at age 50 or 60, you do not have adequate financial protection or savings? Is it too late to improve your situation? No, says Patti Lovett-Reid. When it comes to financial planning, being late to the party is far better than not showing up at all. Lovett-Reid says we all have three ages: our chronological age (how old we turned on our last birthday), our biological age (determined by our physical and mental health) and our financial age (determined by our financial situation). "You can never assume that because two women are 50 years old they have the same financial age," she says. What's more, she underscores the importance of not tying your self-worth to your net worth—a habit that can cause many women to despair.

If you're in your sixties and, like me, do not have enough money to retire on, there are options. Let's explore them.

CUT COSTS

A penny saved really is a penny earned. Financial experts say one important way to sock away more money is to find ways to trim spending. You might do this by eliminating luxuries or unnecessary expenses. Here is where working with a financial adviser can be a huge help. But you may also do this through exploring creative living arrangements, such as sharing accommodations with friends you trust in order to save costs.

FIND WORK

If you have a job, like I do, you may need to keep working longer than you expect. If you don't have a job, you may need to find one. This poses a challenge for women, especially of my generation, who have been out of the workforce for some time. But there are strategies you can use to help you find meaningful work, says Eileen Dooley, a certified coach and consultant with McRae Inc., a Calgary-based outplacement and career coaching company. The first step, says Dooley, is to not lose hope. "I've seen people land all types of roles at all types of ages," she says. If you're early in your job search, begin by making a list of the work you've had that has made you happiest and proudest. Then, list your core values. Both these exercises will help you figure out the type of work or roles you'd be best suited for and would most enjoy. If you have limited paid work experience, take into account any volunteer work you've done, as community-based work is rich with skill-building experiences, she points out.

As you develop a picture of the types of jobs or industries that interest you, it's time to begin networking in earnest. "Networking is the single most important thing you can do to land a job," Dooley says. Make a list of everyone you know who might be able to help you or refer you to someone else: friends, relatives, volunteer acquaintances and so on. Invite them for a coffee and let them know you are looking for meaningful work in the area you have identified. Take time to research industry associations specific to your target industry or occupation and become a member or attend an event. Dooley also recommends researching professional women's organizations, small or large, in your area.

If you're feeling alone, discouraged or uncertain of where to start, hire a coach who specializes in working with older adults. Dooley says, "Why go through it alone?"

If you can't see yourself working for someone else, you might consider starting a small business. More women are starting businesses than ever before, and there are numerous provincial associations and organizations—often affiliated with universities—designed to support new businesses or women in business.

That's what Marney Simmons has done in order to take charge of her financial situation. Building on her experience as an ESL teacher and her years of living in and travelling to foreign countries, she decided to start a writing and editing business helping professionals for whom English is a second language to craft well-written presentations, resumés, cover letters and reports. She enrolled in an online marketing course to learn how to promote her business around the world, and now has clients throughout Canada and internationally. While the business isn't yet earning as much revenue as she would like, it's a start, and this keeps her hopeful.

"I'm creating something myself, and I'm taking positive steps forward," she says.

Unlock the Equity in Your Home

If you truly are at the end of your financial rope, reverse mortgages allow you to borrow money against the equity of your home, without any interest or principal payments. The lender provides you with a lump sum of money, and the interest of that loan is accrued over time and added to the loan balance, which is paid off when you die, sell your house or move out for good.

Reverse mortgages are on the uptick. In 2010, HomEquity Bank, a major provider of reverse mortgages to the over-60 crowd and operator of the CHIP Reverse Mortgage, hit roughly $1 billion in loans outstanding. But the tool is not without its risks. First, interest rates on reverse mortgages are higher than on traditional mortgages. It's possible that the interest rate may, over time, leave you with a mortgage higher than the value of your house. "If people don't have a choice, and they don't have savings, then they may have to unlock the equity of their house. But it's not one of the first strategies we'd recommend," says Caroline Dabu.

As for me, I'm going to keep the equity in my home as a nest egg, and continue working both to maintain my lifestyle and to save for my future. I'm not ready to retire. Financial independence came to me so late in life, I'm not ready to give it up just yet.

CHAPTER 9

A HOME OF ONE'S OWN

Figure out where and how you'll live out the next stage.

I have heard it said that every woman eventually turns into her mother. I never really thought I was like my mum, even though I shared her body type, and her love of children and gardening. I had more of the rambunctious, passionate Sinclair blood in my veins. But lately, as I look at the jars of preserves that line the wall of my pantry, or behold the baskets of fresh fruit that cover the kitchen counter during the harvest, I find myself wondering if I am turning into my grandmother.

When I think of my mother's mother, I always imagine her at home. She lived in a tiny, windswept cottage on the Sunshine Coast. As girls, my sisters and I were sent to our grandmother's house for weeks at a time. She was a poor, hard-working woman, and her home was a fraction of the size of our own in North Vancouver. I adored it. What luxuries she lacked inside she more than

207

made up for with beautiful flowerbeds where there was always something blooming. She had a large vegetable garden. Her cupboards were filled with preserves she had harvested from her own property. She had few possessions, but everything she owned was of the finest quality. There was no excess, no fluff. She lived a simple, pared-down existence. More and more, I'm conscious of a great urge inside me to live as she did.

For a long time, it was unfashionable to talk about anything domestic. The home, with its dirty dishes and unfolded laundry, was an emblem of female subjugation. (And few women were listed on the deeds to their homes.) Though I know that menial household chores are not just for women to do, I have always gained satisfaction from accomplishing small tasks that add to the comfort of my loved ones and me. I seldom have a cleaning person for long; I do not like having someone else muck with my stuff, and I get angry and then have negative feelings about the person working for me. Best just to take care of myself, even if that means I sometimes live in domestic chaos. Often, though, it is bliss. I am a feminist but I have also always been a devoted homebody. No matter where we live—in a little, ocean-facing cottage or a downtown condo—our home represents our place in the world. Home is a critical part of our self-definition, hence our cultural obsession with decorating and landscaping. But my homes haven't been merely a canvas waiting for my unique imprint. They have shaped who I am.

Following Michel's death and the breakdown of my marriage to Fried, I left the dream house I'd purchased following my first divorce. I moved into a serviceable house across the street from Fried so that we could raise Kyle and Ally together as easily as possible. *Serviceable* in this case means horrid. The townhouse was tall and narrow, and huge trees in the backyard blocked the light. It was always cold, no matter how high my electricity bills. I felt miserable in that place. Contrast that awful house to my grandmother's cottage with its commanding ocean view and orderly charm. I always felt safe and happy there, as sure of infinite possibility as I was of the never-ending sky.

As we age, the question of where to live and what possessions to surround ourselves with becomes practical as well as existential. When I was younger, my possessions alternately lifted my spirits and weighed me down. But in advanced age that gorgeous, fading rug I can't bear to part with could catch my toe on a midnight journey to the bathroom and literally be the end of me. And as much as I idealize my grandmother's cottage, that beautiful, remote domicile is an awfully long way from the nearest restaurant (not to mention the hospital). So any exploration of how to live a vibrant, purposeful life after 60 has to include home—where and how to live. No matter where we live, it is the conduit through which we access that most vital part of a healthy and vibrant old age: community and connection.

Samuel Johnson wrote that "to be happy at home is the result of all ambition, the end to which every enterprise and labour tends." I couldn't agree more. The happiest times in my life have had everything to do with home. When Pierre and I were newly married, I counted down the days till we could escape the city for the house at Harrington Lake. It was a huge old country home, surrounded by acres of thick forest on three sides and a deep, dark lake out front. Free of housekeepers, cooks and the pressures of political life, a deep contentment spread over me. I gardened, cooked meals and sewed. The boys were so small then, and on the odd occasions when I had the house to myself, I simply sat and drank coffee and relished the silence. That home was the quiet, solid centre of the universe for my little family, a place where we truly belonged.

The house at 24 Sussex, on the other hand, did not feel like home, though we lived there for seven years. We were never truly alone, for starters. And while I am enduringly grateful for the care shown to me by the staff, and the privilege of living in such a beautiful house, I found it difficult to relax there. I would just settle down with a cup of coffee and a book when in would bustle a housekeeper, ready to tidy an already pristine room. We hosted lavish dinners that required hours of painstaking preparation. Pierre often brought half a dozen of his colleagues in for lunch. I felt like I had to literally stand on guard. And the grand old house at 24 Sussex never provided me with the one thing we want from a home: a feeling of safety.

No matter how old we are, home is both a refuge and a launching pad. It's the place where we can make a mess and leave private belongings lying around for days on end. Home is a place to rest, recover, dream and plan. Our choice of dwelling is important at all times of our lives, and becomes increasingly so as we get older. That's because home is so intricately tied to our independence, as well as our emotional, financial and physical health.

Sally may adore her spacious, memory-filled family home— but does she have the financial and physical resources to maintain it properly deep into her seventies and eighties? Ruth may prize the privacy and anonymity of life in her high-rise condo, but who is around to notice if she falls, breaks a hip and doesn't emerge for days?

As we get older, where we will live becomes a far more practical and strategic consideration. When we live in a place that supports and allows us to be independent, we have less need for advanced care options such as nursing homes. When our homes do not support our independence—either because we are isolated inside them, or cannot care for ourselves properly within them—we sacrifice our freedom and, to varying degrees, our self-determination. There are many choices—the family home, a townhouse, an apartment, a unit in a seniors' housing complex, shared accommodation with friends. The real question to be answered is this: what housing situation will enable us to live as independently as possible for as long as possible?

The Seniors' Housing Crisis

Across North America, we face what many experts are calling a seniors' housing crisis. Housing prices are going up at the precise time our income is going down. Research by the Canadian Centre for Policy Alternatives from the province of British Columbia provides local insight into a national problem. According to the 2006 census, twelve thousand seniors in B.C. spent more than half their income on housing, and 94 percent of them were single women. Of the 20 percent of B.C. seniors who rent, just over half are having difficulty making their rent each month.

This inability to make rent underlines a deeper problem we'll tackle later in this book—the worrying numbers of seniors living in poverty. In B.C. for instance, 14 percent of seniors and 40 percent of single seniors live in poverty, according to the Canadian Centre for Policy Alternatives. Meanwhile, market rent for subsidized seniors' housing in B.C. has gone up 55 percent since 2005. Between 2002 and 2012, the number of seniors in B.C. increased by 36 percent while the number of socially funded housing units, such as retirement and nursing homes, went up by only 2 percent. Because of this, lobby organizations such as the Canadian Centre for Policy Alternatives are advocating for a number of actions to enhance sustainable housing options for seniors. Foundations of this lobby include providing rental assistance, protecting seniors' rights and prioritizing the construction of retirement homes.

I admire these efforts and believe they are worthy of support. No matter where you live in North America, chances are high you know someone who is affected by this crisis of affordable housing. But while group action is vital, we cannot ignore the need to protect our own independence. The first step is exploring and understanding the housing options available to us in our senior years.

Retirement Homes
When we think about housing for seniors, one of the first options that springs to mind is a retirement home. In fact, the term *retirement home*, or *seniors' home*, may refer to a number of different types of accommodation, the personal suitability of which is determined by your preferences, financial means and ability to take care of yourself. If you are unable to live on your own but require only a little daily assistance, you would likely

look for a retirement home. This type of accommodation, sometimes described as social housing, is suitable for active seniors who want to rent their own apartment but share housekeeping, laundry and meal services with other seniors living in the complex. While this is not my personal choice, I know many people who live in retirement homes and enjoy them immensely. Many offer hair salons, spas, shops and workout facilities within the compound.

If you require a high level of care and cannot stay at home, you'd likely look for a nursing home that offers a range of high-level nursing assistance—personal care workers to help bathe and feed patients, for instance. Nursing homes are typically operated by non-profits, health boards, municipalities or private companies. They are licensed and at least partially funded by provincial governments. These types of facilities are normally subsidized, yet seniors may be asked to pay as much as 70 percent of their income to cover the costs. You won't be turned down if you don't have the money to pay for a room in a nursing home, but money isn't the only limiting factor. Given the rising numbers of the elderly and frail, wait lists for these homes are long.

A third and increasingly common option is the private nursing home. These operate much like retirement homes, but offer additional nursing services. These are not usually funded by the government, but in the wake of long waiting lists, they offer those who can pay the option of enhanced care.

I'm comforted to know that should I ever require intensive care in my older age, I will have options available to me that don't require my children to care for me themselves. My mother spent her last years in a private nursing home. It was a clean, bright place, and my sisters and I felt reassured knowing that she was safe. Retirement and nursing homes provide an important and necessary service. Yet, when it comes to nursing homes in particular, experts suggest that we should avoid them for as long as we possibly can.

"Staying at home as long as possible is really the best option," says Susan Eng, vice-president of CARP. When older people are able to "age in place," they retain their independence longer, save on nursing home expenses and are able to maintain their established social and community connections. What's more, Eng and others point out, Canada is unprepared for the rising number of seniors. While wait times for nursing homes are long today, they promise to get worse over time. Not enough social housing is currently being built to meet the demand. The number of seniors living in nursing homes is rising dramatically—up 38 percent over the last decade.

But wait lists aren't the only reason to avoid nursing homes. When adequately staffed with properly trained employees, long-term care facilities have a place—they provide much-needed support for people living in advanced stages of dementia, for instance. But the reality of nursing homes often fails to live up to their promise. As one dementia specialist told me, "They try to be good, but they're awful places . . . they're understaffed."

And in some cases, the staff who work at the home may be inadequately trained to meet the needs of older people. This combination of understaffing and inadequate training can have horrendous consequences for seniors and their families.

In early 2014, a *Toronto Star* newspaper investigation found that hundreds of nursing homes across Ontario were using antipsychotic drugs to calm seniors in the wake of staffing shortages. The paper found that half of all residents were being treated with antipsychotic drugs at roughly forty nursing homes, while a third of all residents were on the medications at almost three hundred homes. If these numbers weren't upsetting enough, many of the medications being used, including olanzapine and quetiapine, were not approved by Health Canada for use by seniors. In fact, older patients who took those drugs were found to have a 60 percent increased chance of death. The investigation also revealed that family members, physicians and at least one coroner had concluded that the use of these antipsychotic drugs was responsible for the deaths of some seniors.

"These drugs are being used to treat a behaviour," says geriatric pharmacist Carla Beaton. "But the real focus should be on understanding what's causing the behaviour." She points out that in some cases, small doses of antipsychotic medication might be a suitable short-term fix to alleviate distress over physical pain and therefore improve a person's quality of life. But it's more important to understand what is causing the elderly person to feel distraught or upset. Pain, needing to go to the bathroom or possible infection can all be difficult to identify in elderly patients, especially if they are suffering from dementia. Beaton says staff must be trained to recognize the signs of these conditions. For instance, while fever is a telltale sign of infection in children and younger adults, fever does not always accompany infection in an elderly person.

More training for nursing home staff is indeed critical, and should be part of a dementia strategy. Retirement homes may be a good option for some, but building a rash of retirement homes across the country isn't going to solve a housing crisis for the elderly, because older adults require a variety of living options—not simply retirement homes. And even if every nursing home in Canada were suddenly and miraculously adequately staffed with caring and well-trained employees, such facilities should still be avoided as long as possible.

"Stimulating environments are best," says Dr. Tony Phillips. Nursing homes—utilitarian buildings often located on the periphery of towns or cities, and home to a relatively homogenous group of people, are less stimulating than housing situations integrated into the life of the community. "We need communities that are designed to facilitate social interaction, stimulate the brain with beauty and nature, and promote exercise," he says. In other words, the fact that you are in your seventies or eighties doesn't mean that you should live in a home where everyone else is also that age and everything is provided for you. In fact, quite the opposite.

Urban planners suggest there are five main elements that characterize the best in sustainable housing for older adults: physical accessibility, proximity to community services, infrastructure that connects housing to those services, a healthy living environment and high-quality social spaces nearby. In other words, ask yourself these questions: Can I easily get into, get out of and move around my home with a cane, walker or wheelchair? Am I close to the grocery store, pharmacy, hospital, nurse practitioner, gym, yoga studio? Is public transportation easily accessible? Is the air quality good? Is there a place I can find entertainment close by? If in evaluating your housing option you can answer yes to all these questions, then you are living in a place that gives you a wonderful chance of living independently.

Another consideration is the accessibility of practical support. To sustain a high quality of life, we need two types of support, emotional and practical, says gerontologist Dr. Amy D'Aprix. "Emotional support—the listening ear and open heart—is actually much easier to come by than practical support," she says. My friends are scattered all over the place. When I have great news to share, or when I feel wretched and need to vent, I can confide in these women as easily by phone as I could if they were sitting in front of me. Practical support, on the other hand, is much harder to find. Practical support is the person who helps you hang the curtain rods, the hands that make you chicken soup when you feel ill, the helper who shovels the snow off your stoop. Living close to people who can offer practical support is in some ways even more important than living close to one's dearest friends. Though perhaps not quite as much fun. Still, as I remind myself during the long Montreal winters, a laugh can be had on the end of a phone line. The snow, on the other hand, simply will *not* move itself.

In my case, I have family members living close by, as well as doormen who keep tabs on the residents in my building and offer security. I have a number of friends who live in town, and we make a point of gathering weekly either to eat together or go out to movies or performances. Developing relationships with neighbours, maintaining friendships and having a list of paid helpers you trust are all ways to ensure you have the practical support you require.

Affordability is another consideration when choosing a home. The sad reality is that few Canadians have saved enough for retirement, and most of us are living on either a fixed or might-as-well-be-fixed income. My home was the right choice when I bought it, but I'm afraid it may not be the right place for me for much longer.

I moved to Montreal in 2007 with the idea of starting over. It was a time of endings and new beginnings. My marriage to Fried had dissolved, and the darkest days of my mental illness were behind me. Ally had been accepted at Concordia University, and I felt a pull to help her through the transition from high school to university life. My struggles had forced her to grow up too fast; I wanted to support her as best as I could. At the time, both Justin and Sacha also lived in Montreal. Most important of all, the newest love-of-my-life was there, little Pierre Trudeau, my first grandson. It felt right to pack up my life in Ottawa—a city that had seen some of my tenderest and most unhappy moments—and start fresh. It was very difficult for me to live in the same town as the ex whom I couldn't seem to let go of.

I knew I wanted to be in the heart of the city, close to the Concordia campus and near my sons. A real estate agent took me around to see a range of condos that fit my modest budget. The proceeds of the sale of my (awful) Ottawa house had given me a small sum of money. And though Montreal is one of the more affordable cities in Canada to buy a place to live—compared to Toronto or Vancouver—I was rather depressed to see the sort of place that suited my price range. Clearly, my Fifth Avenue days were far behind me. Despite my inner shudders over the shabby places I saw, I knew that I was fortunate. Women are far more vulnerable to poverty after age 60 than at any other time of their lives. To have the means to move cities and buy a condo meant I was relatively well off compared to so many. But I couldn't shake the yearning to live in a place that inspired me—even if it was one I apparently could ill afford.

Buying a home is an intensely personal and emotional decision, and when I first walked into my Montreal condo, it was love at first sight. I *adored* the little terrace outside my bedroom (because it was "my" bedroom the moment I saw it). I loved the quaint bathroom with its formidable water pressure and black-and-white tiled floors. The place wasn't perfect, mind you. It required some TLC. But when Sacha pointed out—quite astutely, I thought—that one of the rooms would make a perfect self-contained apartment for a nurse, should I ever need one, I was sold.

My friends tried to warn me off it. Buy this place, they told me, and I'd be signing on to years of soaring condo fees as one refurbishment job led to another. I could hardly afford it as it was, a helpful friend pointed out. Really, they insisted, I should think it through. But while my dream home had rough edges, I felt a sense of *rightness* within its walls. And that was enough to bolster my confidence that I would find a way to make this place work. Besides, I had always lived by the mantra that "money follows"— advice that I now realize is risky at best.

I spent nearly everything I had to get it. Then I spent what

I had left renovating the kitchen and set about making my new home truly mine. I still adore this place, but six years of condo fees later, I'm carefully considering my options. You see, mortgages and condo fees are just one part of the housing equation. As we get older and confront the possibility of declining health (and at the same time try to avoid nursing homes), we must face the fact that we may need to pay for assisted living: home care or renovations that render our homes fit for life as an 80- or 90-year-old. What may have been affordable in our sixties may not be affordable in our seventies and eighties. As much as I love my home, I must find a place that suits my financial reality now and also in the future.

There are many sustainable housing options to choose from. And explore the options I must. I don't want to live in any old *serviceable* place. My heart thrills at the notion of living beautifully, creatively, vibrantly, but also *affordably*. How might I do that? As I dug into the question, I (happily) turned up a number of solutions.

Make Do with What You Have
If you can afford to stay in your home and it fulfills the criteria of sustainable housing for older adults (proximity to services, for example), it's possible that you can simply make do. In fact, an innovative program from Johns Hopkins University is transforming the lives of seniors in the Baltimore, Maryland, area by helping them do just that.

Researchers from the School of Nursing launched the CAPABLE study (Community Aging in Place, Advancing Better

Living for Elders) to determine what basic, cost-effective adjustments could be made in seniors' residences in an effort to keep them out of nursing homes. According to the researchers, most seniors *want* to remain in their own homes. But the loss of their ability to complete "instrumental activities of daily living"—dressing or cooking for themselves, for instance—is the leading predictor of nursing home admission. In an effort to enable seniors to stay at home, the CAPABLE study sends a crew of handymen, occupational therapists and nurses into seniors' homes with a total budget of $4,000 per residence—of which $1,100 is reserved for renovations. While the budget isn't large enough to cover large-scale renos—putting in an extra-wide doorway to accommodate a wheelchair, for instance—it is enough to make myriad little fixes that support independence.

Researchers discovered, for example, that the three main problems affecting a person's ability to live at home include the inability to bathe oneself, to prepare meals and to get up and down the stairs. Installing an additional banister, so that each staircase had two railings versus one, made it possible for subjects to climb and descend the stairs without assistance. Lowering microwaves to within arm's length and installing easy-to-reach shelving promoted cooking. Exercises and stretches—suggested by occupational therapists—made unloading the dishwasher or bending to put casseroles in the oven easier. Grab bars, floor grips and shower seats made the difference between taking standing "bird baths" at the sink and proper bathing. Knobs affixed to the car's steering wheel made driving easier. Replacing patched or uneven floors, and removing rugs or excess furniture, promoted mobility within the home and reduced the likelihood of a serious fall. All these adjustments are small, and most are affordable, especially when compared to the costs of a nursing home or lost independence.

Some parts of Canada offer similar services, while in other parts of the country, we're on our own. But the results of the Johns Hopkins University CAPABLE study are clear—if you want to stay in your home, it's better to make the adjustments you need to make your house safe, comfortable and accessible for years to come.

Find Room at the Inn

What happens if you love your home, but you can't afford to remain there anymore? The following story shows the dangers of staying after your financial ability to maintain a place runs out.

A friend's father passed away recently. He had lived in a large house in a prominent neighbourhood. He was asset rich and cash poor, as the financial people say. He lacked the money required to maintain the house, but continued to live in it for many years as it gradually faded around him.

His children—my friend included—supported his belief that his house would be the financial legacy he left to them. But he should have sold his house years before he did. The lack of upkeep reduced the value of the house. In its heyday a decade earlier, the house could have fetched double what it finally brought in. The amount was nothing to sniff at, mind you, but I share the story because it touches on a concern many people face: what to do with a lovely, big house. As I say time and again, it's always best to know when to exit.

I was discussing this story with a friend when her eyes lit up and she started flapping her hands, obviously bursting to say something.

"Whatever is it?" I asked her.

"The Nantucket Solution!" she replied. "It's brilliant!" And she went on to explain.

When one of her friends found herself in a similar situation—saddled with a big house in Nantucket that she adored, but lacking the money to maintain it—she devised a plan. It all started because one of her closest friends needed a place to live. The friend asked if she could rent one of the six bedrooms in the woman's Nantucket house. Over the next few years, four more people moved in, until every one of the five extra bedrooms was rented. The friends now cook their meals together, share the yard work and support each other in various ways. Best of all, the rental income provides the home's owner with a modest salary and the money she needs to maintain the house so that it keeps its value.

Not everyone wants to open up their family home to renters, of course, even though they might see the benefits of sharing at least some of the costs. For these people, the co-housing model might be especially appealing. First conceived of in Denmark in the 1970s, the co-housing model describes a unique form of community that encompasses both private and public accommodation. In seniors co-housing communities, individuals or couples live in private dwellings while they share public spaces, which may include meeting rooms, living areas or even large joint cooking areas. Co-housing communities are generally built to be accessible, and residents manage the housing jointly. In addition, they pool their money to hire a resident caregiver as needed, and provide help, or "co-care," to each other. Proponents of co-housing suggest that this solution enables people to live independently for as much as a decade longer than if they were living in their own private homes.

My friend Ann and I have tossed around the idea of inviting a group of single friends to pool our money, buy a lot in some charming town or small city and build a commune of sorts, with a central shared living area and a series of private pod-style apartments branching off from the centre. Each pod would have its own parking garage, driveway and entrance. Imagine a spaceship, only tastefully designed (naturally) and constructed from wood. I've also heard about friends who bought adjoining townhouses so that they could enjoy each other's company and also check in on each other on a daily basis.

The idea of living in such close proximity to one's friends might not suit everybody, but we are children of the '60s. If you've tried a commune once—or even if you only wanted to—you can always give it another shot, I say. The beauty of informal shared accommodation is that it enables people to live well and affordably. Depending on who you've got living in the next pod over, it could be every bit as fun, and possibly as adventurous, as it ever was.

Scale Down

Co-housing may not be for everyone. So if you do want to live in your own home, but for financial or practical reasons you choose to leave the family home, an option is to downsize. This is often easier in theory than in practice. And this comes down to the fact that our homes are often a critical part of our self-definition; they represent not only who we are, but also what we have built.

Marg Hachey's transformation from stay-at-home mother and Avon lady to multi-million dollar entrepreneur brought her many rewards, the most cherished of which was her dream home: a 6,000-square-foot Cape Cod–style abode nestled in the Vivian Forest, north of Toronto. The home was a testament to her taste, values and success. The eight-acre property was beautifully landscaped with lush gardens and a custom-made waterfall she could see from her living room window. She had trails cut through the forest and she spent hours in the woods with her grandchildren. The spacious kitchen was outfitted with a four-metre-long island and lots of comfortable seating. "I could cook, entertain and never miss a thing." She even installed an in-home theatre—fitting perhaps for the CEO of a company that provided audiovisual service for Queen Elizabeth II. "That home was my creative canvas. I loved it," she says. Marg and her husband figured they'd stay in their dream home forever.

But within a few months of each other, first her husband and then Marg herself developed cancer. After a long and challenging recovery, they came to the difficult realization that they didn't have the physical wherewithal to maintain the sprawling home. They needed an easier life. In short, they needed to downsize.

As a businesswoman, Marg had made hundreds of difficult decisions. Leaving her dream house was different. "It was incredibly emotional." They put their house on the market expecting it would take months—or even years—to sell. It was gone in two weeks. Within a month, Marg and her husband found themselves in a 2,000-square-foot single-level home on a golf course, in a community populated by many people also in their sixties, seventies and even eighties. The house is spacious and comfortable, and life is indeed easier. All the landscaping is taken care of by the developer. In winter, the snow is cleared from their driveway and steps by six a.m. There are security patrols, and nearby neighbours provide an additional layer of security. There are frequent social gatherings, nearby amenities and a restful golf game is as close as her back door.

Possessed by Possessions

Many of us will have to downsize eventually—whether to a smaller apartment, a co-housing facility or a seniors' home. When the time comes, one of the most difficult tasks may be dealing with decades' worth of possessions.

I was flipping through the TV channels one evening a few months back when I chanced upon a program about hoarders. I watched in morbid fascination as a woman about my age guided a camera crew through her unspeakably cramped home. From the street, the house appeared to be an average 1980s-era split-level with a paved driveway, brick porch and fading white siding. The inside, however, was straight out of a horror movie. The countertops, shelves and tables were covered with stacks of magazines and folders and plastic bags filled with who knows what. In the living room the furniture was barely visible because it was all loaded down with garbage bags full of old clothes, extra sheet sets and assorted junk. The place was dark, dingy and horrifying. When the commercial break came on, I snapped off the TV and willed the nausea that had overcome me to subside. When I could manage it, I sneaked a look at my jumble of boxes and Tupperware bins stacked untidily in "the corner": a smallish nook off my living room that had gradually become my own miniature version of a hoarder's paradise.

After that one episode of *Hoarders*, I've never allowed myself to watch another. Hoarding is a bona fide mental illness, related to obsessive compulsive disorder. Some people suffer from the illness acutely, like the woman I watched on TV, and others have a milder strain—so mild, in fact, that you would hardly call it an illness. If a friend were to walk into my apartment, her eyes would likely skim right over "the corner" and think little of it. In our "buy lots, buy cheap" society, most households are drowning in stuff. But now when I look at "the corner," a little shudder runs through me because on the one hand, I know I have to deal with the contents of those boxes; on the other hand, I absolutely don't want to.

Extreme hoarding aside, I know that most people have problems dealing with clutter. One explanation is our consumerist culture, but the tendency to hang on to possessions goes much deeper than that. We cling to possessions for three main reasons: we think they may be useful in the future, they are emotionally significant or holding on to them gives us a sense of safety. The problem is that so many of things that make us *feel* safe are actually delusions. A bad marriage, a toxic friendship, nightly snacks of sugar cereal with warm milk. In the same way, stuff we hold on to can become an albatross. I likely would have started fresh years before I bought my Montreal condo if it hadn't been for the basement of my dreary little house in Ottawa.

Before the dreary Ottawa house, I lived in the dream house that I bought after my divorce from Pierre. It was a spacious, comfortable house with four bedrooms, a big warm kitchen and a generous, leafy garden. I lived there for twenty years, but downsized after the end of my second marriage. Therapists and life coaches often say that the state of a person's house mirrors her interior life. The dreaded house in Ottawa perfectly reflected mine at the time—dark, inhospitable and cloistered. And this external environment not only mirrored my mental state when I moved in, but also, I feel, reinforced my depression for much longer than if I had been in a brighter, more hospitable place.

When you downsize from a big house to a small house, you end up with a lot of stuff you no longer have space for in the rooms you use for everyday living. Which is how my basement came to contain a stack of boxes containing the boys' old clothes, toys and schoolbooks, ancient skis and snowshoes, forgotten books and other paraphernalia of a full family life. The boxes tugged at me each time I went down to the basement. I knew I should deal with them, but it felt like a Herculean task. I was still seeing my psychiatrist regularly in those days and each time I visited him I'd end up talking about the boxes. They were my nemesis. Part of me was afraid to sort through them; I knew Michel's boyhood belongings would be in there and I couldn't bear seeing them. Nevertheless, having his stuff packed away in boxes beneath my roof made me feel as though he were still close to me. But it was a false comfort. My boy was gone.

I began to avoid going down to the basement altogether. And whenever I had thoughts of selling the house, I'd remember the boxes in the basement and how I'd need to deal with them. And so the months and then years wore on and a stack of cardboard and a pile of possessions kept me in a house I truly hated far longer than I should have been. I couldn't move forward because I couldn't make decisions about how to leave behind the past. All I could do was moan about the boxes. When I eventually bit the bullet, bought the condo, sold the dreary house and started to pack, the process of sorting through the boxes was far easier than I had thought. I got through them in a day. You see, it wasn't the stuff itself that held me prisoner. It was the unhealthy attachment I'd cultivated to the stuff.

I got rid of a lot of my belongings when I moved into the condo, but soon after I moved in, little piles of clutter began to sprout up again, and not just in "the corner." Some of these I had deep emotional attachments for—the stacks upon stacks of family photographs, for instance. But there was a lot of my stuff that I hadn't yet parted with not because I loved it but because it was valuable. The pink flower-rimmed bone china dinner set for twelve, for instance. I offered it to Ally, but she wrinkled her nose, said it wasn't her taste and that she'd prefer a plain white set from Canadian Tire. (She may have a point: little pink flowers on plates have been done to death.) But whether Ally wanted my china or not, something had to be done. As my mind got clearer, my instincts, which I have learned to trust, were urging me to cull. And quickly.

I have always had lots of energy, and still do. But I know that energy will not last forever. The time to get rid of stuff is now. The father of a dear friend passed away recently, leaving his three children—all in their sixties, with various health complaints—to sort through the mountains of possessions he held in his 2,500-square-foot home. Grief, in my experience, is best done over bowls of hot soup, a few choice photo albums and contemplative walks. Sorting through ancient junk drawers, hauling mothball-scented winter coats down from the attic and boxing up cupboards of empty Mason jars does not enhance the process.

The funny thing about possessions is that the things that held so much meaning when a person was alive usually lose their sentimental value quickly after that person dies. In the days after her father passed away, one friend told me, she didn't want to part with anything. Three years later, she has some photographs, a handful of books and his old fishing rod.

I don't want to burden my children with my stuff, nor do I want to be schlepping boxes when I'm 80. Inspired perhaps by *The Best Exotic Marigold Hotel*—a film about a young East Indian man who remakes a failing hotel in India into an apartment complex for Brits of a certain age—a friend of a friend is considering building a retirement community in India. What if I decide *that's* the place where I should spend the rest of my days? I couldn't possibly cart the entire contents of my 1,000-square-foot condo to the subcontinent, and I am far too practical to pay to store things I neither use nor love. What's more, I'm aware that we often use our stuff as our protection or armour against the world. More and more, I feel a calling to simplify, to let go of belongings and just be me.

I developed a little mantra to help me with the indecision that swept over me each time I held up an old serving platter, stuffed animal or book. It is actually a rhyming phrase I learned from my mother: *Keep the best, get rid of all the rest*. Because the tendency to hang on to possessions is so engrained, and each item feels meaningful in its own way, decluttering is an act requiring great willpower. And the trouble with willpower is that we start off the day with a vessel of the stuff, but it is quickly depleted. (Hence my frustrating habit of resisting sweets all day long, only to cave to a bowl of sugar cereal before bed.)

As I sorted through the basement boxes, I asked myself whether it was the best in its class. Was it *really* among my best serving platters, or was it merely good, or worse, *serviceable*? Only the best made it to Montreal. Another decluttering strategy is to do it in short bursts—focusing on one small area each day and then moving on.

It's tempting to hang on to family heirlooms, for instance, but I simply don't have room for all the trinkets. Instead, I've kept certain items that encapsulate an important piece of my family's history. For instance, my great-times-five-grandfather, William Farquar, was a Scottish-born British officer in the East India Company who played a pivotal role in the founding of Singapore in the early nineteenth century. While there, he commissioned various Chinese artists to illustrate local plants, animals and insects. Copies of several of the original 477 paintings hang in my guest bedroom, as an homage to my adventurous ancestor.

I also keep a few select objects that trigger powerful memories. Reliving happy times has been shown to increase happiness, and provide an overall boost to one's mental health. Rather than post family portraits around my house, I have carefully selected pictures that jog my memory about happy times. There's one I keep in my bedroom, for instance, of a tanned, bare-chested Michel playing hacky-sack with a circle of hippie friends. I see that photo and I celebrate the fresh-air-loving, free spirit he was. It makes me smile.

I'm not on any urgent deadline anymore. I have no imminent move. So rather than exhausting myself sorting through my possessions, I'm taking the slower, methodical approach. I am gradually going through my condo, shelf by shelf, identifying the best of what I have, and giving the rest away, to family members, the Goodwill, or, when no one wants it, to that final resting place of possessions that have outlived their use, the city dump. I have also instigated a new wardrobe rule: *One thing in, another thing out.* Despite my manic bouts of over-shopping, I'm not the sort of person to come home with handfuls of bulging shopping bags. My mother drilled into me and my sisters the idea that it is better to buy one fabulous piece of clothing versus a bunch of clothes that are less expensive but of poorer quality. I have saved some of my best vintage outfits for my daughter, but nowadays, if I buy a new blouse, I force myself to get rid of an older blouse before I can hang the new one in my closet.

Down with Downsizing

When you reach a certain age, there is tremendous pressure to downsize. On the one hand, this makes sense. Cull your possessions, simplify your life, tread lightly. And yet, there's something about the smugness with which downsizing advocates extol the benefits of living small that provokes my inner rebel. The notion

I don't like is that getting older should automatically mean living smaller.

Nancy lived well within her means for many years. She, her husband and five children shared a discreet, elegant family home, one without pretension but filled with fine art and lots of laughter. During the winter ski season, they all squeezed into a 1,000-square-foot apartment in Whistler. When Nancy and her husband retired, they decided to trade in their pint-sized urban footprint for a sprawling existence. They purchased a 250-acre farm in the countryside just north of Toronto and built their dream home, complete with a bedroom for each of their grown children. Yes, it means that much of the house stands empty most of the year. But on the rare occasions when everyone's holiday schedules align, they can live together comfortably as a family—complete with partners, and one day grandchildren as well. As much as the idea of maintaining a large house tires me, I do love the idea of having a large, inviting gathering place for my five children and their families. The other option, of course, is to live beside one of my children in a quaint granny flat with a private entrance and soundproofed walls.

The important thing for me, and for you, is to carefully consider our options sooner rather than later. Despite new building codes that have improved the accessibility of new homes and buildings, Canada, like most other developed countries, is woefully unprepared for the tide of aging baby boomers. We must safeguard our own happiness and independence in old age. We can't control what will happen to us in our senior years, but we can prepare as best we can by dealing with our possessions and planning where and how we will live.

The truth is, I'm happy in my little condo, for now at least. The doormen help me hang pictures and install curtain rods, and it's comforting to know there's someone downstairs who would notice if I didn't come out for a few days. I'm two blocks from the hospital and a short walk from the trails at Mont Royal. Two of my children live in the city, and two more a few hours' drive away. I am happy and comfortable here for now. But I will keep culling the clutter in case a room ever opens up in that seaside house in Nantucket.

CHAPTER 10

LEARNING TO LIVE WITHOUT

Through the process of facing grief and loss,
emerge stronger and more resilient.

All good things must come to an end. And the end of this remarkable experience on earth is death—our own death, and the passing of people we love. When we are younger, if we are lucky, death
feels like something very far away. But as we grow older, and as
the people we care for age, death becomes more imminent; we
have so many more years behind us than we do ahead. And so
we must ready ourselves for what is coming. Death and loss are
subjects few people enjoy discussing, but preparing ourselves, I
would argue, is an essential activity of our third act.

Understanding Grief
My life has, sadly, forged in me an intimate relationship with grief
and loss. Despite the contentions of some that death is a normal

part of life, and we need to simply "get over" our losses, my experience has been that we *never* get over losing the people we love. Never, ever.

According to Dr. Marie-France Rivard, the loss of a child is the most painful of all for a woman. I can attest to this. My grief for Michel is no longer unbearable, but I continue to think of him each day, and often when I remember him, I experience a fresh stab of pain that he is lost to us. But years of therapy, deep reflection and conscious healing have transformed my initial despair into "clean pain"—a pure form of sadness that is free of the feelings that can complicate grief, feelings such as anger, regret or shame. It was not always this way. The truth is I struggled mightily with grief. So much so that Michel's death very nearly became my own.

In the aftermath of Michel's drowning, my family and friends gathered around to support me. I was crushed by the loss, but in the days and weeks immediately following his death, there was nothing unusual about that depth of despair. I had just lost a son. Of course I was distraught. Gradually, the frozen lasagnas and cards and visits began to drop off as friends and family members returned to their normal lives. But my despair continued, wearing me down and crushing me beneath its weight. The sadness locked me in a dark and selfish universe. I couldn't offer any support to my other sons and daughter, all of whom had lost their wonderful brother, because I was utterly consumed with my own grief. I shut myself away from other people—I didn't think anyone could understand how I felt. I wanted to be alone in my sadness. And besides, I wanted to be alert for signs from him—messages from my darling son that he was with me, still close even in death. And so I turned down invitations from girlfriends to go for coffee dates or walks or evenings at the theatre. I felt swept off the ledge of life.

There was one friend who stayed by my side, however. She brought me soups and fresh bread every couple of weeks. It is a testament to the state of my despair that I sometimes found it hard to be grateful for her visits. I wanted to be alone, and she kept disturbing me with her soups! But her dogged visits provided me with nourishment for my body and spirit. And she was the one who finally alerted my family—themselves wrapped up in sadness—and also told me, ever so gently, that my grief was not normal. That I was in trouble.

Doctors diagnosed me with post-traumatic stress disorder. Ultimately, this PTSD triggered the massive mental breakdown I experienced in 2000. Drugs helped me regain my mental balance and intensive counselling helped me right my thinking. But grief hung over my shoulders like a mantle I couldn't shake off. I was recovering my health, but I was still preoccupied with the memory of Michel. I simply had no idea how to let him go. Indeed, I felt that I saw him every day in the form of a young crow that perched on a branch near the window of my house in Ottawa. One day, when Justin was visiting, the crow flew into the house and became trapped there. I looked on in shock as Justin shooed him out. So deep was my desperation that part of me wanted that bird to stay in the house forever.

You see, crows and ravens hold meaning for me. In the 1980s, Pierre, our boys and I went on a trip to visit Haida Gwaii, an archipelago off the coast of British Columbia also known as the Queen Charlotte Islands. Pierre was made a Raven Chief, our boys, Children of the Raven, and I, a sister of the Eagle. Seeing this big crow (whom I thought of as a raven) perched outside my window day after day comforted me because I felt Michel was giving me a sign. I believed he was telling me that he was there, that I was not alone. I woke up each morning and searched for that raven/crow, and seeing the bird lessened my grief. I have since learned that this behaviour isn't unusual. It's common for the bereaved to look for signs of their departed. Following the death of her husband, a woman I know swore she heard him in the calls of an owl that hooted outside her window. But looking back, I see that my preoccupation with the raven was a sign of my own delusion and desperation. After losing someone we cherish, what we want more than anything is to believe that they may magically return to us. Even in a non-human form.

My mental breakdown and the ensuing therapy instilled in me the importance of right thinking—taking the time to carefully examine our thoughts. As much as I wanted this raven to be a sign, as tightly as I clung to the idea of my son being close, I knew that this line of thinking would only bring me more suffering. Looking back, I see that my anguish had become "unclean." A Buddhist proverb teaches us that "pain is inevitable; suffering is optional." The pain I felt over losing Michel was an intense fire I had no choice but to walk through. Isolating myself in my sorrow, and deluding myself that he was still here on earth sending me signs, prolonged my time in that fire of grief; it caused me to suffer far more than I needed to. And so I resolved to get help.

Over the years I had volunteered as a fundraiser for the

Wabano Centre for Aboriginal Health in Ottawa. I have always held a deep respect for Aboriginal people, and no matter where I have lived, I've tried to maintain a connection to Aboriginal organizations. One day I confessed my ongoing grief to a friend, who suggested I pay a visit to Sister Irene at the Wabano Centre. The idea felt deeply right to me, and so I did. On the day of my appointment, she brought me into a small, simple room that looked very much like a room in which might one visit a massage therapist. I lay down on a narrow bed in the centre. Sister Irene was a lovely, plainly dressed woman with a wise face, seeing eyes and a long, silvery ponytail. She sat in a chair by my head and asked me to tell her why I had chosen to come and see her. As I spoke, she held her hands over my body, slowly moving them as though performing reiki. As I got further into my story, my grief overtook me. I sobbed, and still she moved her hands around me, chanting as she did so. At some point, I fell into a sort of trance. I felt a great pressure inside my chest, an expansion and contraction like the beating of wings, like a sort of birth. I felt something stretching and expanding inside me. And in my mind's eye, I saw a raven leave my body, hover in the air above us and fly away through the wall.

I was in Sister Irene's office for almost two hours. When I got up to leave, I felt woozy and light-headed. But my body was lighter than it had been some time. I had been holding memories of Michel inside my body for years. I had been so petrified by the depth of my grief that I had held on to him. But we cannot hold on to our departed, no matter how sad we are to have lost them. I had to let Michel go. Sister Irene's healing helped me to do that.

What I felt conscious of in that darkened room was that Sister Irene was taking me through a ritual—a grieving ritual that dates back generations. I had gone through therapy, I had regained my mental balance, but I had not gone through a ritual of grief. Our culture has so few remaining rituals around loss. We used to take on mourning clothes, make hair shirts, bathe our dead, dress them lovingly and take pictures of them. Those traditions are largely a thing of the past. And though I would not like to wear black for a year, I will acknowledge that ritual is a powerful alleviator of grief. In a 2013 article for *Scientific American,* Harvard University behavioural scientists Francesca Gino and Michael I. Norton point out that rituals performed after experiencing loss relieve grief. In one of their experiments, they asked people to write about the death of a person they loved, or the end of a close relationship. Some people wrote about rituals they had performed after the loss. They found that the people who had performed a grief ritual experienced less grief than those who did not perform a ritual but only wrote about the loss.

In their article, Gino and Norton point to the work of anthropologist Bronislaw Malinowski, who lived with and studied South Pacific islanders. He found that before these people went fishing in dangerous and shark-infested waters, they performed specific rituals that they believed would invoke magical powers to protect them. When they went fishing in placid waters, they didn't perform any rituals. His conclusion: we humans use rituals when we encounter situations in which "the outcome is important and uncertain and beyond [our] control."

Facing the enormity of carrying on when someone you

cherish has died—especially when that person is your child—is just such an instance. I needed Sister Irene's ritual to help me face that uncertainty. And by engaging in that ancient ritual, I also tapped into the universality of grief. In a way, rituals help to normalize grief. Rituals remind us that while grief is experienced as a deeply isolating pain, it is in fact a quintessential part of the human experience. It has been described as the price of love and the cost of commitment. It is an emotion humans have always known, and one that we become ever more familiar with as we age.

Normal Grief

There can be nothing "normal" about losing someone you love and cherish. And yet, all of us who experience loss go through a series of universally experienced stages. Five stages of grief transcend cultures and socioeconomic background, says Elisabeth Kübler-Ross, a Swiss-American psychiatrist, in her groundbreaking work *On Death and Dying*. Under "normal" circumstances—such as when a person's grief is unhindered by underlying mental illness, as mine was—the bereaved person goes through five stages of mourning: denial, anger, bargaining, depression and acceptance.

The first reaction to learning of the death of someone we love is usually some form of denial and isolation. This stage lasted a long time for me—I kept waiting for some miracle that would bring my son back to me. I isolated myself from my family and friends because I didn't want to expose them to the depths of my grief, nor did I feel they could come close to understanding what I was going through.

Anger usually comes next—often because we can't take the continuing pain, and so we redirect and express it as anger. In my case, I felt furious at my sons for committing me to the Royal Ottawa Hospital. I turned my anger toward them rather than acknowledging the real cause of my distress.

Bargaining is the third stage—an insidious reaction to the helplessness we feel, and an attempt to regain control. Often this happens in the form of "if onlys"—*if only I had done this or that to prevent Michel from taking that fateful ski trip.*

Depression comes next—an overarching sadness that precedes the final stage of grief, which is acceptance. This is what my time with Sister Irene helped me to achieve. Only once I had accepted that Michel was gone from this earth could I release him—and myself—from the dark cave I had created. And with this acceptance came the return of hope. I started to believe that life might be good again. My sense of humour returned—I began making jokes, trying to make people laugh. I remembered that the world was not only a painful place, but a beautiful one. And I was still alive within it.

One of the world's first attachment theorists, psychologist John Bowlby, described grief as an experience parallel to an infant's response to being separated from its mother. He described how when a baby is separated from its parent, an inner motivation system is triggered, moving the child to do everything it can to regain its mother's closeness and care, to retain a sense of normalcy. Through the grieving process, the bereaved woman reorganizes her life in a way that allows her to return to a state of normalcy over time.

When Grief Isn't Normal

There are no rules around grief. A friend told me once that after she lost her father, her (very young) doctor told her that she should begin feeling better within two to three months. I have never experienced such a speedy recovery. The stages of grief, and indeed the process as a whole, are unique to the individual. In a 2004 research paper published in *Advances in Psychiatric Treatment*, psychotherapist Andrew Clark describes different types of what psychologists describe as "pathological grief"—instances in which the natural human grief process is hindered in some way. In *inhibited grief*, there is an absence of grief symptoms at any stage. It is as though a person's grief has been put into a box and set aside. The grief is there, but the person simply won't allow herself to feel it. This is common, Clark writes, among people who see expressing their feelings as a sign of weakness, and so the person experiences "too little" grief. *Chronic grief* happens when a person experiences "too much" grief, and this is common in situations where the bereaved had an overly dependent relationship on the person they lost. Clark goes on to describe signs that distinguish a major depressive episode from "normal" grief:

- feelings of excessive guilt
- thoughts of death
- feelings of worthlessness
- psychomotor retardation: a slowing down of thoughts and movements
- hallucinations

I experienced many of these things following Michel's death. There were times when I truly wanted to die. I was so lost and filled with despair that I simply couldn't see the beauty of all the things I have to live for. I will be forever grateful to my friends, family, counsellors and dear Sister Irene for helping me through the grieving process.

The Stages of Change

There is one thing that has truly surprised me about grief and loss: I was not prepared for the fact that after I walked through the fire of grief, I would emerge, like Lazarus, a different person. And in many cases, the version of me that each successive grief experience forged has been stronger, more resilient and more self-determined. "It's a part of grief that people don't often talk about," says gerontologist Dr. Amy D'Aprix. "It is a sense of freedom that can emerge after someone we love has died." Dr. D'Aprix says that people who know us intimately—in particular our parents—hold us in a certain regard. "Every relationship has a set of invisible expectations and bonds" that, to a degree, become a part of our assumed identity. When that person dies, those expectations can fall away, which is at first frightening, but also freeing. It is the process of grief, Dr. D'Aprix notes, that helps us re-articulate that sense of who we are. For instance, in the immediate aftermath of my mother's death, I felt sad and bereft. After all, she had been the adult. As long as she was alive, I was someone's child. But as I worked through my own sense of grief, I emerged a subtly but profoundly different woman. Now *I* was truly the adult, with no parent to turn to anymore.

And this brings me to another useful sociological model with which to consider grief. Some years ago, Dr. Martha Beck developed a matrix that describes the cyclical nature of psychological change. According to Dr. Beck, we are always resting somewhere on a continuum of change—meltdown, reformation, emergence and full flight. Catalytic events—like the death of a loved one—throw us into a state of meltdown. Our idea of who we are as a person is radically altered, and our sense of self breaks down. This meltdown stage represents the entire process of grief, as our vision of who we are—mother, wife, sister, daughter—"dissolves." Dr. Beck's advice during this stage is to take our lives one day at a time and take care of ourselves by literally cocooning with soothing cups of tea, warm baths and blankets around our shoulders. Counselling and gathering with others who have experienced the pain of personal dissolution are also helpful.

As time passes and the grief subsides, we begin to re-form— gradually we're able to imagine possibilities once again. Eventually, we emerge from this phase and begin to act upon our dreams and imaginings. And ultimately, that action brings us to the final phase of the change cycle: full flight. There we remain until another catalytic event—the loss of another loved one, a new job or a move—changes our sense of identity yet again.

Our connections and relationships are not only the foundations of our lives and happiness—they are also part of what makes us who we are. When we lose someone near to us, we also lose a part of who we are, and thus we must re-form ourselves. This is an aspect of grief that isn't talked about much, but acknowledging this cycle of change is a key part of the process.

Understanding the grieving process is crucial in preparing for loss. But there is much more we can do. As we age, we must strengthen our relationships in order to cultivate the support we need.

Nurture Your Relationships

Relationships with close family and friends take on new significance as we age. That's because we face the loss not only of people we love, but also of our own independence. And because social isolation is such a major risk factor for many health problems, maintaining our relationships becomes more urgent as we get older. Alas, families can be complex. If you do have difficulties in your relationships with your children or loved ones, now is the time to resolve them, says geriatric psychiatrist Dr. Rivard. "Get help early," she says. "If there are interpersonal difficulties with people who are going to be important to you and your life, seek out counselling services to help you resolve those conflicts."

Even if you have strong family relationships, the realities of older adulthood can strain them enormously, says Resa Eisen, who in addition to her work as a family therapist is the founder—along with Dr. D'Aprix—of the Essential Conversations Project, a facilitated process that helps families discuss and prepare for the challenges of older adulthood. "There are so many transitions at this stage of life and all of them are very significant," says Eisen. "As you age, your dependence increases and your independence decreases." From selling a house to making a will, the decisions we make at this stage of life affect not only ourselves, but also the people close to us. And this interdependence can create all sorts of family problems, says Eisen. The thing is, they almost always start out innocently.

For instance, she describes a situation in which two grown daughters—both of whom lived a fair distance from their parents—believed it was time for their aging parents to move into a retirement home. The parents, however, felt they were still capable of living at home and would not consider moving because they would not be permitted to bring their beloved dog with them. Over time, misunderstanding and misalignment began to break down into frustration and even hostility as each side felt the other wasn't listening. By taking the family through a facilitated discussion process, Eisen was able to engage each member in discussion, help the family lay the issues out on the table and ultimately make some decisions and plans that were mutually acceptable.

One of the factors complicating these important discussions is the resurrection of long-buried "issues." "It's all about who got the red truck," Eisen jokes. "Wounded feelings, who Mom loved best, unresolved conflict . . . all these things come to the fore." What distinguishes mediation and essential conversations from therapy, Eisen says, is mediation's focus on getting critical issues on the table and working toward resolution. "A mediation deals with fairness," she says.

This type of mediation can be especially useful when older adults are preparing or reworking their wills, she says. "It's important to have these conversations early." Finances, end of life care and wills are all vital discussion topics, says Eisen.

In my experience, many people understand, intellectually at least, that such discussions are valuable. So what holds so many families back? Often, a reluctance to have these essential conversations comes down to one of two things: either a family member doesn't wish to face the pain of imminent loss, or he or she doesn't want to bother other family members with his or her problems. Eisen relates a situation in which a woman in her late sixties, who was diagnosed with the early stages of Parkinson's disease, confided that she didn't want to burden her two grown daughters with a discussion about her future care. "The problem is that if they didn't have the conversation, they were going to be far more troubled because they wouldn't be prepared."

Research has shown that when these discussions happen early, outcomes are usually better for everyone, especially as compared to discussions that happen *during* crises—say, immediately following a death or the loss of some significant ability. Eisen says, "People who are in crisis often feel very disempowered. They don't feel confident, clear, organized or satisfied. They're fearful." The preparation that comes from proactively discussing loss and transition can help all parties feel better prepared and less afraid of the changes to come.

Consider Your Legacy

In the face of so much loss, it's easy to become hyper-focused on what we don't have, or the things we stand to lose as we age. And while it is crucial that we spend time preparing for these inevitabilities, it is also important that we take time to consider the legacy we want to leave.

"Taking stock of their lives and understanding their legacy can be the heart of the emotional work people do in their later years," says Dr. D'Aprix. Spend time thinking about what you value most, and what is truly meaningful to you. This will help you prioritize and decide how to spend your remaining time, and how to allocate your estate. One excellent exercise Dr. D'Aprix suggests is to create an "ethical will." In this document you write down the stories, experiences and values you want to leave behind for your friends and family. Collecting pictures and photos, and taking a stab at writing a short (or long!) autobiography or family memoir—these activities are also fun, and they help us to honour and celebrate a life well lived.

What is my legacy? What do I most want to be remembered for? There are so many things. I hope my family and friends cherish my joie de vivre. I hope they remember my sense of humour, and invoke it when they experience the inevitable difficulties that life presents. But above all, the legacy that I want to leave is the overarching importance of acceptance. To learn to see, accept and love what *is,* is one of the defining lessons of my life.

CHAPTER 11

CELEBRATE LIFE

Honour the distance you have travelled.

Tragedies can only be endured while they are in progress—the more you try to escape the pain, the worse it is. There is no out-running the inevitable storms of life; you can only move through them.

The gift of getting older is that we can look back and gain understanding of the triumphs and the tragedies, large and small, of our lives with a depth that we might not have been capable of when they happened. Simply put, age gives us an opportunity to reflect. The third act is all about drawing meaning from the seemingly disconnected storylines of our lives. And when I look back on the narrative of my life so far, I see the fullness of the human condition. There has been love, pain, excitement, boredom, pride, humiliation, hope, disappointment. It's all there, as rich, fortifying and flavourful as a cup of freshly brewed espresso.

Many writers have commented on the powerful draw toward memoir as they age; they, like I, feel an almost daily desire to contemplate and connect the dots between the disparate elements of our lives. I have a little terrace outside my bedroom in Montreal. I fill it up with flowers and herbs in the summertime, and sit out there in the mornings enjoying my coffee. It is totally private, walled with flowers and terracotta pots. And as I sit here, listening to the sounds of a bustling city, yet somehow separate from it all, I think about life. What is the connection among six decades' worth of story and experience? In a word, *spirituality*.

Contemplating the Big Questions and exploring spirituality is, I believe, part of the great work of our lives as we push north of 50. Don't get me wrong. I'm not advocating a big, boomer rush on the church doors. Nor am I suggesting a pilgrimage to India (although that does sound like fun). What I'm suggesting is that we all regard the third act as an opportunity to explore the deeper meaning of our lives.

I grew up going to Sunday school, as so many people used to do. Our family said grace on special occasions and we all professed to believe in God. But I had a casual relationship with religion until I met Pierre. He was a devout Catholic and I admired the certainty and strength he drew from his faith. I converted to Catholicism before our marriage. He never explicitly asked me to, but I sensed that adopting his religion was an unspoken expectation. I promised to raise our children in the Catholic faith and did my best to adopt it as my own.

The trouble is, the more I learned about organized religion, the more questions I had. And inevitably, these questions led to trouble. I remember a trip Pierre and I took to Italy to visit Pope Paul VI. The pope was staying in his summer residence at the time, a sprawling villa on Lake Como. We had hit a rough patch in our relationship and Pierre thought it might be helpful to seek counsel. So I carefully prepared some questions I wanted to ask, and on the day in question, readied myself as painstakingly as if I were meeting—well, the pope. I remember holding tightly to the banister as we climbed an enormous palatial staircase to the room where the pope would receive us. He greeted us warmly and he and Pierre began talking. I don't recall exactly what these two world leaders discussed, but I do remember feeling the discussion was never-ending.

Finally the pope turned to Pierre and said, "My son, do you have any questions for me?"

"No," Pierre said, "my faith is solid."

Then he turned to me. I drew in my breath, ready to ask him my questions—whether it was truly possible to sin in thought, his thoughts on abortion and on birth control. But I never got my chance. He put his hand out to bless me—a gesture that at the time felt an awful lot like I was being silenced.

"I understand you have three beautiful sons," he said.

"Mm-hmm."

He smiled radiantly. "Surely you are blessed among women."

And then we were dismissed.

I was livid. I stomped down those elaborate stairs so hard I was sure I'd break them. Meanwhile Pierre, who'd gotten a kick out of the whole thing, teased me and asked if I'd gotten the answers I needed. Of course I hadn't. I felt belittled and humiliated. But looking back, I see that my audience with the pope taught me a lesson: that I would not find the answers I was looking for in organized religion. I would have to search for them elsewhere.

One of the great blessings of my life is that I have had the chance to meet so many influential people, including religious leaders. Some years ago, Sacha and I had a private meeting with the Dalai Lama. I remember that he took my face in his hands and said, "Margaret, you are the mother of the world." Wow, I remember thinking. Some mother. I was initially bewildered by what he told me, but I think of his words often, especially when I do my work as an advocate for women's rights, clean drinking water and mental health. That is my mother-of-the-world work.

As much as I loved the Dalai Lama and as frustrated as I was with the pope, my brushes with religious leaders have taught me that, at the end of the day, they are just men. Powerful men who lead movements that are also institutions. And while there is a lot to be said for organized religion, no matter how devoutly you follow a school of thought or a set of beliefs, at the end of the day, your relationship with the divine is something that happens within you. *You* find and define it.

For me, any authentic discussion about spirituality always, always leads me to a single theme: love. You might call it God. I think of that power as a great energy, and that energy is love. And love is patient, generous, kind, compassionate and still. I savour that stillness each day when I meditate. Meditation isn't easy for me; one of the consequences of bipolar disorder is a racing mind. So every day, four or five times, I do micro-meditations—a few minutes of deep breathing, where I draw in new air to still my tired mind. And in that stillness of meditation, I feel something profound inside me. And what I feel is love.

In fact it was a Jesuit priest who captured my religious philosophy most accurately. Father Regis taught Pierre when he was a little boy, and became our confessor priest when we lived at 24 Sussex. Once a month on a Tuesday he would come for dinner and afterwards he'd listen to our confessions. He got to know me very well.

One day he took me aside and said, "Margaret, we're all trying to get into the state of grace. What we need to understand is that we are already there. You've already got it. You just have to live it."

Father Regis was referring to that peaceful love I feel inside me when I meditate. A calm, expansive energy that is always there, always waiting. I can see the wisdom of his words now, though I didn't see it as clearly at the time. Because a few short years after that conversation with Father Regis, I embarked on one of the most selfish, self-preoccupied and narcissistic phases of my life. I was lost and hated myself for being lost. I was disconnected from my family and hated myself for that too. You could call the months after I left Pierre my days and nights in the desert. I once regarded that phase of my life with shame. But today, when I look back on that younger woman, I feel only tremendous compassion. If only I had taken Father Regis's words to heart. The light was inside me the whole time.

What I do admire about organized religion, however, is its emphasis on ritual. Rituals are a powerful reminder of the sanctity of life and of the human condition. I still go to mass from time to time, but these days I make my own rituals. Except I don't call them rituals. I call them celebrations.

When I take stock of my life, the events I recall most vividly and fondly are always the times I have celebrated with the people I love and cherish. If grief and loss are the price of love, celebration is love's festive companion. To this day, I frequently host Sunday dinners at my house—gatherings of family and friends where we eat meals that have been lovingly prepared and revel in lively conversation.

In a life marked by episodes of tragedy, celebration is the way in which I honour the life that others have lost. It is my way of cherishing all that is sacred about this experience: kinship, food, conversation. Celebration is the way our family has healed from the devastation of losing Michel and Pierre. It is how we honour their memories and each other.

Our biggest celebrations always seem to happen at the cottage at Morin-Heights. Sacha and my beautiful daughter-in-law Zoë married there a few years ago. We had a dance floor in the backyard, a stage for a Malian band and a tent village for guests. The next morning I went for a walk to the stream where the priest would be christening little Pierre later that day. I found Sacha in his underwear with a tool belt round his waist. He was putting the finishing touches on a massive deck and walkway he'd built specifically for the christening. That's my Sacha, industrious and hard-working, and capable of building anything. Pierre was christened in the stream, with dozens of our closest family and friends—and his newly married parents—surrounding him. We all cried tears of joy; and in that moment of celebration we didn't mourn what we'd lost, we celebrated what we had.

The older I get, the more these moments mean to me. They are a reminder of how far I have travelled, and how much I have to treasure in this life.

ACKNOWLEDGEMENTS

First of all, I would like to express my sincere gratitude to my core team: Iris Tupholme, senior vice-president and executive publisher of HarperCollins Canada, Hilary McMahon, executive vice-president of Westwood Creative Artists, and Eleanor Beaton, my editor and researcher. Thank you, Iris, for believing I had another book in me. Thank you, Hilary—your cheerful yet sound advice kept me on track. Most important, thank you, dear Eleanor, for diligently editing my seemingly endless stream of words and researching the themes in the book with insight and respect.

I would like to thank my friends Ann White, Nancy Self, Christine Shacken and Vicky Wilgress for their stores of huge life changes they faced. Ann is a professional photographer and she accompanied me on a WaterAid Canada study tour in Mali in 2014. With her camera, she caught me dancing under the noonday sun with exuberant women and children who had just learned that WaterAid Mali would be coming to their village to offer clean water and sanitation. I was feeling the joy and gratitude myself, and Ann snapped the shot used as my author photo for the book jacket. (Thank you, Terry, at theprintlab.ca, for not removing my wrinkles.)

To all the experts, thank you for your knowledge. The more we know, the better prepared we are for what's next.

Thank you to my dream team at HarperCollins Canada: Leo MacDonald, Noelle Zitzer, Doug Richmond, Neil Erickson, Alan Jones, Colleen Simpson and Cory Beatty. Special thanks to freelance editors Allyson Latta and Sarah Wight.

This book would not have been possible without my wonderful agent at Speakers' Spotlight, Mélanie Roy. Your tireless support is invaluable.

Finally, huge thanks to my grandchildren: Pierre, Xavier, Gala, Ella-Grace, Ariane, Amelia and Hadrien. You give me the will to live in the best way I can.